Ginny —

You and John were so connected to Rotary and the motto "self above self." You live by that motto throughout your life, giving and helping others. You have a wonderful family who continue the service to others and always appreciate that commitment. With great love and respect.

My best,
Bill

William J. Miller

P.S. Best wishes and enjoy the read!

| Praise for The Politics of Prevailing |

"Dr. Miller, based on his extraordinary career serving 42-years as a school district superintendent in one school district, shares "better than fiction" stories he experienced throughout his distinguished career in which he persevered to transform the district into a high-performing, highly efficient model that other superintendents, boards and district leaders should learn from and replicate."

Jim Buckheit, Executive Director, Pennsylvania Association of School Administrators

"A compelling and interesting presentation of the high and low points of one man's lengthy and crisis driven career in public education. A good read."

Joseph F. Bard, Executive Director, Pennsylvania Association of Rural and Small Schools

"There is no greater supporter of equal opportunity for ALL children in the Commonwealth of Pennsylvania than Bill Miller."

Arnold Hillman, Pennsylvania Association of Rural and Small Schools

"This is a personal, hard-hitting reflection on the vast array of experiences encountered by Dr. Miller during his more than 40 years in the Tyrone Area School System. Dr. Miller takes the reader through the exhaustive and sometimes contentious situations that he faced with all phases of the educational system-school boards, politicians the general public, parents, students, teachers and the teacher's union, A must read for all who are interested in becoming a public school superintendent!"

Frank Rosenhoover, retired PSEA UniServRep

"*The Politics of Prevailing* presents an illuminating and real-world review of the many challenges faced by school administrators, as well the challenges confronting our education system generally. Dr. Miller provides a unique perspective, through his and his father's many years of service to the Tyrone Area School District and the obstacles they faced during their tenure, and he offers insights into effective leadership that make a fascinating read not only for school administrators, but for all of us who care about the issues that arise in our schools and how those issues should be addressed."

Michael J, Betts, Betts Law Office LLC, Pittsburgh, PA

"An insightful look into the world of a long-term successful superintendent, Dr. Miller doesn't pull any punches when relating encounters with difficult individuals and the problems they've created for schools, and he's very forthcoming describing the principles and strategies he has employed to overcome them. A refreshing and enlightening account for experienced and aspiring superintendents alike."

> *Dr. William T. Hartman, Professor of Education, Pennsylvania State University*

"This writing is a concise account of the long tenure of an effective and respected superintendent. It is not an account of research-driven higher education, but rather it opens the door to a talented human being working in that often overwhelming role of public school leader. The author, Dr. William Miller, is that long-tenured and often-tested superintendent. This writing can guide new and veteran school leaders to patience and to a better practice of complex school leadership."

> *Dr. Lawrence Weiss, Executive Director, Pennsylvania School Study Council, Pennsylvania State University*

"*The Politics of Prevailing* is an insightful reflection of a very successful, but challenging superintendence. Dr. William Miller "prevailed" throughout a forty-two year tenure by recognizing early on that public education in our democracy is a political endeavor. Developing political savvy as he navigated through a myriad of challenges he held tenaciously to his core values and his focus on what was most important to the children he served. His writing style is very much that of narrative story-telling, as he shares the episodes of many years as a successful superintendent and encapsulates them in a series of lessons learned."

> *Dr. Brian M. Small, Executive Director, Shippensburg University School Study Council*

"In his book *The Politics of Prevailing,* Dr. Miller provides a real life chronology of how to survive the transformation of being an instructional leader to becoming a political broker. Clearly, the role and duty of the superintendent have been usurped by renegade school board members, teacher strikes, declining enrollment, school closings, civil rights issues, court interference, and the loss of basic subsidy. These changing trends have not adequately been addressed in graduate schools nor in required in-service programs. Therefore, the seasoned superintendents with long tenure must fill the void by sharing their knowledge and experience. This is exactly what Dr. Miller provides in his book. A must reading for all novice and veteran administrators."

> *Dr. Dennis Murray, Superintendent, Altoona Area School Districts, Retired [1984-2013]*

The Politics of Prevailing

Lessons in Public School Superintendence 1971-2013

Strategies for Meeting Change and Challenge with Confidence

DR. WILLIAM N. MILLER

Mechanicsburg, PA USA

Published by Sunbury Press, Inc.
50 West Main Street
Mechanicsburg, Pennsylvania 17055

www.sunburypress.com

For information about special discounts for bulk purchases, please contact Sunbury Press Orders Dept. at (855) 338-8359 or orders@sunburypress.com.

To request one of our authors for speaking engagements or book signings, please contact Sunbury Press Publicity Dept. at publicity@sunburypress.com.

ISBN: 978-1-62006-623-2 (Hardcover)

Library of Congress Control Number: 2015951465

FIRST SUNBURY PRESS EDITION: September 2015

Product of the United States of America
0 1 1 2 3 5 8 13 21 34 55

Set in Bookman Old Style
Designed by Crystal Devine
Cover by Lawrence Knorr
Illustrations by Scotti Everhart
Edited by Celeste Helman

Continue the Enlightenment!

For my wife Melissa, who wrote me the hall pass allowing me to be married to my job and for her willingness to give up the many missed summer vacation trips over the last four decades. And for superintendents everywhere—particularly the one who came before . . . and the Normans who follow.

Contents

Acknowledgments

I am indebted to the tens of thousands of students, parents, employees, administrators, and board members whom I had the privilege to serve over the years. In particular, I treasure the loyalty of Tanya Sharer, my secretary and confidante of 29 years; the faith of Board President Tony Androski; the school board members who were willing to support a 29-year-old kid by turning the reins over to him; the leadership of Board President Willard Hickes and Harry Sickler, whose commitment to the board and community was as exhaustive as that of Board Presidents Lee Stover, Larrie Derman, and Jim Crawford, who guided the district through critical periods in its history; and the endurance of Marjorie Barr, who served as business manager from 1971 to 1993. Likewise, I cannot fail to acknowledge my parents Dr. Norman and Catherine Miller for their love and unwavering support. Therefore, all earnings from this book will be directed towards scholarships in their names to benefit economically disadvantaged students as they attend a technical school or college of their choice. Last but not least, I wish to thank my wife Melissa Miller; my children Norman Miller, Veronica Miller Colegio, and Fred Miller; and their families, along with the many dogs and cats that have shared our lives—all were there for me when I needed them.

Foreword

A Word about Shoes

They were black size-twelve Florsheim wingtips.

As a kid, I was fascinated with the classic brogue pattern stippled into their fronts, their shine as dependable as the leather fragrance that stuck around no matter how often he wore them. My father had a pair in every color—buckskin, taupe, Bordeaux, oxblood, chestnut, burgundy, saddle, even white for after Memorial Day. He was a frugal man in every regard, but he was a meticulous dresser—and shoes were his indulgence.

On a rainy summer afternoon, my sister and I decided that it would be amusing to dress up in our parents' clothes, so while she smeared lipstick on her face in the bathroom, I slipped into my father's closet and tugged on an Oxford dress shirt that hung to the floor. Choosing a navy tie, I squinted into the mirror and fashioned a misshapen nub that was a few loops shy of a Windsor knot. The lopsided ends that swung precariously below my thin ankles were an afterthought.

And then came the wingtips, their formal blackness oozing manhood from the soles. I took a few steps in them and was transformed. I was a five-year-old magnate itching to do man-things, like read a newspaper, smoke a cigar, or tilt back a glass of bourbon with branch water. I was so smitten with this virile persona that when my sister called out "You ready?" from the bathroom, I jumped entirely out of the Florsheims, tripped over the tie, and landed in a basket of dirty underwear.

As I would rediscover twenty-odd years later, my father's shoes were incredibly hard to fill, but as Dr. Norman Miller's three decades as Superintendent of the Tyrone School District passed, the board of directors considered passing the reins to me. My father taught me much about human nature. He taught me respect for differences, principles of motivation, patience, work, integrity, and forgiveness. From him I learned that a man who works with his mind is no better than one who works with his hands, that honey catches more flies than vinegar, that success demands endurance more than speed, and that giving is more meaningful than taking. Even though my father had groomed me with sage advice and practical values for over a year, I still recall preparing for my first board meeting, trying to mold a navy tie into a respectable Windsor, making sure my shoes were tied, and hearing somewhere from the distant reaches of memory my sister's voice calling out: "You ready?"

And I knew at that moment *who* I was, even if unsure how ready I was. I knew that with the grounding of my father's lessons and a decent pair of shoes, I could be the man that I admired in him. During the next forty-two years, when it seemed like there might not be another year to serve, when the balance sheet was zero and when my entire administrative staff was on the chopping block, I could look into a mirror and see a five-year old kid with skinny ankles floating in size-twelve shoes, and I knew it would be okay. I was fortunate to have in my father an accessible mentor. Without his mentorship, I doubt that I would have made the journey through the first two years, let alone the subsequent forty. Mine is a story of prevailing through changing times, and this book is a legacy of mentorship for all who aspire to serve and to lead our schools.

The lessons are simple. Ignore them, as I sometimes did, and you too might step into a basket of dirty laundry.

Preface

As superintendent of a small Pennsylvania school district, cradled among the farms and hills of the Allegheny Mountains, I navigated five decades across what may have seemed to careless observers to be relatively tame political waters. By the time I relinquished the helm of superintendent in 2013, the Tyrone Area School District with a pre-K to 12 enrollment of 2,000 was a vessel of fiscal and educational efficiency. The district's students graduated from high school during the last two years of my service with the highest cumulative value-added academic growth rating in a state of 543 brick-and-mortar and cyber school districts. Collectively, in reading, writing, science, and math, our students outperformed even elite suburban schools whose students had the advantage of per-pupil expenditures more than double those of Tyrone's. Our schools had been honored multiple times as one of "America's Best Schools" by *U.S. News and World Report*, classified as "Outperforming" and "Beating the Odds" by Standard &Poors School Ratings Services, and used as a case study of excellence by the Education Commission of the States. Amazingly, the district maneuvered these feats with a waif-like property tax burden and an equalized millage rate in the state's bottom percentiles—an unparalleled educational return on investment—a team accomplishment which students, teachers, parents, administrators, community groups, and school boards worked tirelessly to achieve. Make no mistake—a feat like this cannot be undertaken alone. In fact, it demands so much teamwork that I feel remiss about using the word "I" at all in this book except when contextually necessary.

Despite our fiscal and educational successes, however, all sailing was not smooth over the span of my decades of service. The daily operations of the district were beset with crises that were specific to a rural, economically challenged population; our struggles were often to maintain a balance between our region's core values and an approximation of the best practices in education that we could afford. With each decade, as was typical with most public school districts, political and economic snares emerged from both local and national sources, entangled operations, and forced us to act decisively, to marshal support from diverse constituencies, to evaluate solutions—and perhaps most importantly —to retrench behind our personal values. On occasion, these snares resulted from lapses of personal judgment—more on those snafus later. However, our adherence to core values—advancing student literacy skills, transparency in operations, maintaining our mission amid cultural changes and shifts—served us well. That, coupled with our ability to understand the often couched local politics and context of each situation—guided the district through the storms.

Near the conclusion of my years of service, we were fully immersed in the political game of the 21st century, lobbying and educating Harrisburg legislators drunk on the questionable claims of *Waiting for Superman*[1] and the half-truths of taxpayer-funded cyber education ad campaigns. We braced both the community and staff for a free-fall over a fiscal cliff (precipitated by a nationwide withdrawal of federal funding) and into the maw of "radical efficiency"—as Penn State public education finance expert Dr. William Hartman dubbed the survivalist mentality needed to weather 13% annual budget cuts while producing growth. We struggled against the tightening vice of No Child Left Behind, generating superior results from staff with(until more recently) lagging compensation.

All of this transpired with harmonious labor relations in a state that led the nation in teacher strikes for over a decade. Our staff braved the monolithic rise of cyber schools that devoured increasing swaths of brick-and-mortar funding every year, generating neither resignation nor doubt, but instead a new professionalism, a client-provider model, and a vow to outperform the competition. Without hesitation, we reacted swiftly to disasters simmering beneath the surface of sexual allegations against staff members; we protected children with minimal disruption to the mission of the schools. We also confronted public backlash at the decision to shutter neighborhood schools so that the district might consolidate all children at one campus. This process was

---

1 A controversial documentary film released in 2010 by director Davis Guggenheim. It celebrates the charter school movement while presenting an impassioned indictment of the American school system and teacher unions for much of what ails public education. The film was lambasted by many authorities (including Diane Ravitch, former assistant secretary of education under H.W. Bush, she currently is serving as research professor of education at New York University, and Rick Ayers, author and academic scholar) for lack of accuracy, void of addressing larger issues affecting student performance, and a "slick marketing piece full of half-truths and distortions."

intended to erase glaring gaps in instructional opportunity and quality while eradicating the routine hardships placed on itinerant personnel such as our library, art, music, special education, and physical education teachers. Having all teachers at one base meant increased efficiency for staff, a richer curriculum for kids, and significant financial savings by consolidating four elementary buildings into one campus.

While most of these political conflicts informed my later years, none of them had the impact of two pivotal battles in my formative years: one with a Ponzi scheme that nearly paralyzed the district's ability to make payroll in the throes of the largest construction project in its history, the other with a coalition of ultra-conservatives who threatened to do away not only with a curriculum of classics like *Of Mice and Men* and *Fahrenheit 451,* but also with eight key staffers, including the man at the top. Perhaps it was my baptism-by-fire with these two formative battles that made later encounters with politics comparatively routine. I approached the office with the presumption that conflict was a prerequisite to change, not a pathology of leadership.

Through all of these challenges, I clung to a clear understanding that superintendence was by nature political, a reality that, according to Barbara Loomis Jackson in *Balancing Act: The Political Role of the Urban School Superintendent,* many superintendents face grudgingly. As Jackson posits, "Trained in the tenets of an ideology that defines conflict as pathological and consensus as . . . legitimate, superintendents may find conflict more painful than other executive officers. A defensive, hostile response to criticism may then generate more intensive conflict." Jackson could not be more on point, as the narratives in the following chapters illustrate. Political conflict is a regular part of a superintendent's breakfast—and it's a breakfast served cold for far too many. What characterized my superintendent's career with the Tyrone Area School District was a sense of constancy and my perceived need for continuity in an economically disadvantaged area. Many, however, as this book details, named my decades of service following those of my father a dynasty rather than a tenure of commitment. Yet it is the lack of continuity in superintendency that has been named a major problem in the profession. As the Education Commission of the States declared as early as 2001, "the superintendency is in a state of crisis," with the average tenure of a superintendent lasting slightly over five years in many states. A 2003 report by the Education Writers Association blames part of the crisis on "the need to understand and be adept at the politics of the job." This need to play politics was as much a reality in each chapter of my career as was the need of each child in our economically disadvantaged community to receive the best education that limited funds could buy.

Our story is one of stakeholders on a national, state, and local scale threatening the district's mission with competing values and needs—most of them fiscal, some ideological, a few criminal, but nearly all personal. Throughout the lessons, there are numerous individuals who I have referred to by using pseudonyms and certain identifications of several elementary schools. I want this book to be a story of object lessons for the prospective leader as much as it is a story of the frailties and desires of human nature and how, at our best, we may strengthen and transform that nature for the greater good. It is a spiritual story—and, I hope at least to some, an inspiring one—of the political snares of the office and how steadfast values and political savvy can serve and prosper society's most vulnerable members—its children.

"The first test of a truly great man is his humility. By humility I don't mean doubt of his powers or hesitation in speaking his opinion, but merely an understanding of the relationship of what he can say and what he can do."

—John Ruskin

1 | Eat Humble Pie

As Ruskin postulated, the true measure of leadership is not the arrogant application of power as much as it is the keen awareness of limitations. Imagine if modern politicians and other public figures adopted Ruskin's stance when rightfully accused of breeching power or violating policy. Rather than face a legacy of infamy, reviled political and sports figures like Richard Nixon and Barry Bonds might have salvaged enough dignity and public empathy with a heart-felt admission of guilt in order to live another professional day and enjoy productive careers. Instead, the natural instinct—and the most arrogant one—is to mobilize the damage control or to engage in a cover-up. What follows are two parables about how I tried to maintain an awareness of my own limitations. In doing so, my course of action was publically to admit guilt, or at least to concede error. Then and now, the results proved to be the most ethically sound—and I contend—the most politically advantageous.

The May 21, 1997, headline in the *Tyrone Daily Herald* spelled it out clearly enough: "TASD Superintendent Accused of Violating District's Political Policy." I had erred in circulating a nominating petition for incumbent school director George Field to teachers and staff on district grounds during a school in-service day. The prevailing political conflict at the time was between board incumbents who were perceived by local religious zealots and challengers as the liberal education establishment intent on doing damage to our students' souls. In reaction to my politicking, press-hungry board challengers soon ran the following quarter-page advertisement in the local paper, replete with the Jerry Falwellian overtones so reminiscent of the decade:

OUR NATION IS IN A MORAL DECLINE
TYRONE IS IN A MORAL DECLINE

Our Superintendent, William N. Miller, and our School Directors violated School Policy #321 —"Election petitions may not be passed or distributed on school property or during school time. The Board may dismiss the administrator who violates this policy." The administrator was William N. Miller.

Is campaigning one of the requirements on Bill's job description? We don't think so. We feel Bill should be DISMISSED and billed for the time and energy spent campaigning for these incumbents.

On Tuesday, May 13, we presented the violation to the board at the regular school board meeting . . . You know he is the "professional." Not one, we repeat, NOT ONE school board member wanted anything done about his violation.

Just remember this VIOLATION when you receive a notice from the school district that your child is being punished or expelled from school. WHAT IS GOOD FOR THE GOOSE IS GOOD FOR THE GANDER.

MAKE YOUR VOTE COUNT ON TUESDAY, MAY 20 —VOTE FOR [BARB]&[JUDY], **SCHOOL DIRECTORS.**

Perplexed about the appropriate disciplinary action against me, then Board President Larry Derman solicited advice from Pennsylvania School Board Association's Chief Counsel Stephen Russell, who suggested that that the board had, among other options, "the option of doing nothing." However, after some real soul-searching, I recognized my over-reach in circulating the petitions. I quickly made the decision easy for Mr. Derman by confessing to *Herald* reporter Mark Leberfinger that "Obviously it was a stupid thing to do, the petition could have been completed without me . . . It was done on the spur of the moment. I should have waited to do it at night or on weekends . . . I obviously apologize."

I also revealed to Leberfinger that my all too human motives were guided partly by a reaction to challenging candidates who harbored a vendetta about our school consolidation plans reaching back almost a decade earlier. At that time, this plan involved a shuttering of beloved neighborhood schools, particularly the higher income Friendship and Elizabethtown Schools[2]. This consolidation was intended to produce optimal growth and opportunity for all district students and to negate economic disparities that were producing measurable differences in student achievement. Eventually, the consolidation effort produced the achievement-gap closing results that we had envisioned.

At the time, however, my ardor over the consolidation issue also eclipsed my better judgment. It was in 1989-1990 that the Barb and Judy coalition, attempting to derail board candidates they perceived as aligning with me in school consolidation, began in earnest. With passions running so deep, it makes little sense for a superintendent to disguise an affiliation with a candidate who espouses his ideals, so I did not hesitate to place election signs on my lawn supporting board members whose vision and open-mindedness I embraced. I realize that most superintendents embrace a publicly laissez faire philosophy that allows them an objective credibility on the matter of their boards. So although the battle had been fought over an entirely different issue nearly a decade earlier, as is often the case in public and private life, karma was asking me to pay the price in the form of my 1997 violating activism.

In taking full measure of my mistake, I reminded Mr. Derman that a first offense for a staff member probably would not result in a letter of reprimand but rather a stern warning and a reminder of duties and responsibilities. Nonetheless, to underscore for both the staff and the public that I wanted not to abuse my power but to act from a position of humility and contrition, I asked Derman to reprimand me—to place a letter in my personnel file. In taking public responsibility for my overreach violation, I not only wanted to model public humility and responsibility, but also to signal that we needed to put this issue to rest. We had vital work to do—work that could be derailed by conjuring up old political ghosts.

---

2 Pseudo names used for identification of elementary schools in the district.

I can look back now with mild amusement at still another incident that may have been a career-ender for a superintendent who might conceivably be rattled into an arrogant, cover-up posture. Although I did not violate a policy in this second instance, having the humility to state the truth clearly and calmly while confronting the press was paramount to maintaining both my human vulnerability and my ethical credibility as a public figure. Here is how I ate humble pie again.

I was lunching in the high school vocational restaurant, The Eagle Inn, when a receipt that I failed to see fell out of my pocket. A student worker retrieved the receipt, which was, as luck would have it, not one from my recent trip to the hardware store but one for a gag gift purchased on non-school time at an adult novelty store in honor of my good friend's fortieth-birthday party. (This fact was later substantiated by the board upon further investigation.) The student dutifully turned the receipt over to his teacher, who delivered the receipt to me. I went out of my way several times to meet with both student and his parents through contact with his teacher to explain the situation, although those meetings never occurred. I wanted to reassure them that all was well, that the student should have no fear of reprisal, and that my out of school purchases did not, in fact, violate my on the job legitimacy.

What ensued over a course of days and weeks as a result of my week-end foray into an adult novelty shop threatened to devolve into a scandal that some perhaps hoped would cost me my job and that others saw, fortunately and ultimately, as a non-issue. Despite my efforts at transparent damage control in this incident, after news of the receipt got into the hands of a board member on the night of a school board meeting, I soon received a call from a reporter at the *Altoona Mirror*. According to the reporter, an anonymous letter sent to the board had also been copied and sent to the *Altoona Mirror* stating, that "This act on the part of Dr. Miller is scandalous and unacceptable for a school administrator. Please investigate this and take appropriate action. This is a Christian community and this behavior cannot be tolerated."

As the drama unfolded, I was visited by two Pennsylvania State Police troopers who came into my office to warn me that the board member was "out to get me" and intended to pursue my purchase as "criminal and illegal," despite the troopers insistence that it was not. They informed him that it was perfectly legal and that by no means should police time be wasted on the matter. The board member then called the school's attorney and the

Pennsylvania School Board Association. Anticipating a local newspaper feeding frenzy around the rumors of salacious behavior on my part, I also attempted to talk candidly with then editor of *The Altoona Mirror* as a way to avoid such headlines and media gossip. Ultimately, the school board's own lawyer, Cynthia A. Yeager, reported the following to Board President Lee Stover on July 15, 2011, underscoring that the purchase was made on my own time and thus disconnected from my work performance:

> Unless there was some connection between Dr. Miller, the purchase, and . . . [his] work performance, it would appear the incident was not actionable . . . It is clear, I have determined, there is no legal basis upon which to pursue this matter. Yeager also indicated that board members or others intent on pursuing the matter further might open themselves to potential litigation.

Approaching a potential crisis calmly, as I did in these two cases, is by no means easy. The instinct to protect and defend one's public reputation might restrain the more proactive and honest desire to admit publically and humbly one's missteps. But politically speaking, complete honesty and calm humility are paramount. Superintendents will make mistakes—too many to count. Few days went by on the job that I was not reminded that my feet were made of clay.

Years ago, a Tyrone elementary teacher who later became superintendent at another Pennsylvania school district conducted a survey for his doctoral thesis on factors affecting a superintendent's longevity. Recently, I dug through some old shoe boxes and file folders and rediscovered the survey responses of our staff that were produced as anonymous reflections on both my effectiveness as a superintendent and on the work environment in the Tyrone district. The survey asked teachers and other staff members to respond to a variety of questions, among them items such as this: "In describing your superintendent's long tenure in this district, to what personal qualities or professional skills would you attribute his longevity?" Or, another example: "In general, describe the type of work environment within the district."

As I dusted them off, I recalled that not all were flattering to my tenure at TASD, producing yet more humble coming to terms on my part. For example, one respondent claimed that "rarely does our administration truly collaborate with teachers. Administrators decide what they want, and then they inform us." Another staff member, who obviously had no memory or experience with the anti-Miller school boards from the 1990s, claimed that I "have the ability to charm whichever school board member he happens to be dealing with." Some of my staunchest board critics might have choked back laughter on that one, though they were not always known for their sense of humor. In fact, I encountered considerable political resistance around even non-controversial or advance research-proven programs—like all-day kindergarten in the early 1980s, with some parents expressing fears that the spiritual and emotional influences of the home might be undermined in the pursuit of earlier academic training.

Yet many of the comments reflected an acknowledgement of what I considered to be one of my genuine leadership strengths: that part of my success was the mentorship I received from my father, who preceded me as superintendent at Tyrone: "His father was also a great business mind and he learned much from him," an individual wrote. Perhaps the most pleasing to me was the following, which focused on what I liked to believe was my unflagging devotion to our district: "[He] is dedicated to this community and was not using this position as a stepping stone to anything else. He knows this is where he is happy and successful. There is a lot to be said for that."

There are elements of truth to be found and lessons to be learned from all of this feedback on my service, both positive and negative. But one stood out for me more than all of the others. A teacher had this to say when asked what quality accounted for my longevity:

> I feel many people do not know the real Dr. Miller. They see the Superintendent. I have seen the person that he is. If he is with others as he is with me—and I assume that he is—he is approachable and wants you to see him as a person and not just your boss. He will visit my room and talk to my kids and they love talking to him. Just ask yourself, 'How many superintendents will get down and tie a kindergartener's shoe?'

And that is where longevity in this game begins—with a kindergartener's shoelace. If we adopt an attitude that puts the needs of children above our own, then whenever a $26 million dollar operation may be at stake, the political fight is not to preserve our own skin but to preserve the future for thousands of young minds and souls. The battles that I recount in this book were not fought by me alone nor for me alone but for the thousands under my watch.

From that humble vantage point—of getting down on the knee —we summon the will and energy to engage in decades-long political battles. With humility, the least confrontational and most contrite response possible can help a school leader avoid the meaningless media circus and keep the focus where it needs to be, namely, on providing quality education to kids who need it.

Principles of Prevailing

- ✓ Leadership is not the arrogant application of power as much as it is the keen awareness of limitations.
- ✓ Admit guilt when guilty. Do not mobilize the damage control team or engage in a cover-up.
- ✓ When innocent, do not hesitate to vindicate your name.
- ✓ It makes little sense for a superintendent to disguise an affiliation with a political candidate who espouses his ideals—but do not over-step school policy.
- ✓ Urge the board to deal with you *more* severely than you would deal with a staff member.
- ✓ The least confrontational and most contrite response possible can help you keep the focus on providing quality education to kids.
- ✓ Tie a kindergartener's shoe.

"A desk is a dangerous place from which to watch the world."

—John Le Carre

2 | Ditch the Desk

I n business management it's called MBWA, or Management By Walking Around. Your clipboard can be empty. Just carry it with you, perhaps with a pencil stub behind the ear, and the high visibility of authority will ensure both accountability and productivity.

I cannot recall many days when I did not at least once abandon the security of the desk. Behind the desk, it is easy to believe that all the important work of education is being faithfully executed by those you personally had a hand in hiring and empowering through a judicious delegation of duties, in the end validating your superior, even clairvoyant reading of human nature. Your principals will manage efficiently. Your teachers will plan imaginatively. Your custodians will clean meticulously. Remember, micromanagement is no virtue. You're the architect of a highly productive work force.

That's just about when the roof falls in. And in September of 1997, that is literally what threatened to happen. The district had invested $26 million dollars with Devon Capital Management through its financial advisor John Black, who was recognized throughout Pennsylvania as an expert in his field. But after our literal and metaphoric roof caved in, what we later discovered, according to state officials, was that those funds had been placed in unauthorized, high-risk investments with the money now reflecting a market value of less than half of the district's initial investment. So in the middle of a massive roof and mortar reconstruction of our buildings, we were left with only 12 of our initial 26 million plus to work with.

Most of the money we were using was derived from municipal bond sales for the intended building projects: the new PreK-5 elementary complex and the renovation of the high school. With a new building under construction and a high school in stages of renovation, a significant investment had already been committed to the projects. The district had only $400,000 in the bank to meet all general fund operation and construction costs. There was no other source of funding when the district assets were frozen. Although it was not readily available yet, for the short-term we were told that we could count on a state debt-service reimbursement payment of roughly two to three million dollars that would be coming our way.

I had always made a point of being a vigilant leader without micromanaging affairs. I literally walked the district, visiting each building regularly just to keep my finger on the pulse, speaking to all the stakeholders, understanding the complexities of morale, getting to the truth first-hand. Before the day the construction fund laid a goose-egg, I perceived getting out from behind the desk as a preventative measure, not a rescue effort. Neck deep in a construction project, with roofs and conduits in some buildings exposed to the elements, with staff to pay and kids to educate, I knew instinctively that the desk and I would not be seeing much of each other. In truth, footwork like I had never experienced before would be the only way out of the morass.

Over the next year, as we attempted to recover lost monies literally to keep our district up and running, Business Administrator Cathy Harlow and I would travel the state, especially frequenting the state capital in Harrisburg scores of times. Calmly but passionately, Cathy and I tried to convince state legislators to restore tens of millions in lost funds. This was no easy task, as many in our own community, especially political rivals, blamed Cathy and me for the loss. To political rivals, the Devon Capital Management case was not fraud at all. To them, it was at best a colossal failure in financial oversight; at worst, it was a risky gamble undertaken at the expense of public funds devoted to children. Nonetheless, we pressed on, seeking reductions in fees from contractors and architects, making them aware of the district's position. We were successful in at least one endeavor, as our architect agreed to reduce his fees by $25,000.

My legwork, though, began at the desk, for sure. An initial report by the trustee appointed to handle the case recommended a resolution to the loss of funds that would have paralyzed the district. Immediately, with the help of staff, we assembled hundreds of pages of documentation: a cash flow analysis, a delineation of all our schools and their varying states of dilapidation, and a chronology of events from the building consolidation plan, ranging in time from the inception of the building plans to the eve of the Devon investment loss. Through endless hours of clerical and administrative labor, we chronicled a host of monetary self-help initiatives to show in good faith that we had attempted to restore some funding, but that there would be no way that the district could function again without a life-line from the state.

State Senator Jubelirer's aide, David Atkinson, saw my face in his office almost every week during this two-year process. When we first showed up with our massive documentations, Atkinson seemed incredulous that we had followed through with his recommendation to compile the hundred-plus pages of various documents, so thorough was it in detailing our crisis. We sent copies to other districts such as, North Lebanon, Daniel Boone, etc victimized by the fraud, so that they could plead their cases for loans, though their papers were far less exhaustive. We also conducted a termination versus completion analysis to demonstrate that doing nothing would be a more costly alternative, with millions of construction underway yet partially completed. If we did nothing to actively seek a remedy or to convince the Governor and legislature to understand our dire situation, all would be lost.

At the time, the state was funding a baseball stadium only fifteen miles south of Tyrone along Interstate 99. We used our awareness of the state's "generosity" in funding this enterprise as a point-counterpoint argument for asking them to also to share some of the state largess in aiding our educational plight. Perhaps this paragraph from the February 19, 1998, position paper that I delivered to Governor Tom Ridge's cabinet, which included the Secretary of Education and legal staff, captured best the gravity of the moment:

> If distributions are made to school districts in accordance with the Trustee's original report . . . the Tyrone Area School District could lose almost $12,000,000 due to the alleged fraud case. The incredible loss, if permitted to stand, will destroy the educational system and the community of

Tyrone. While we applaud the state grants for economic prosperity in the southern area of Blair County with funding for a multi-million dollar convention center and professional baseball complex ($28,000,000), the Tyrone Area School District will suffer in economic despair. Property values will decline and our children may be forced to remain in unsafe and insecure buildings that should be vacated. On the other hand, our children may move into new and renovated buildings while local taxes are raised outrageously without concern for the citizens of an economically depressed school district . . . Without state assistance or state grants, the students and community will confront economic ruin. We desperately beg you to consider assisting us in this fight for survival.

To rally support for no-interest government loans, I regularly traversed the state, logging tens of thousands of miles, armed with binders of material and the prodigious position paper. Especially important to the cause were hosts of letters from community leaders like Dr. Kathryn Lewis, who implored U.S. Senator Arlen Specter to support the School District Loan Act, and Dr. James Ramsay, who petitioned Senator Robert Jubelirer to recognize the inadequacy of the financial solution cobbled together by the Ridge Administration—one so impotent that it barely recognized that the crisis was caused by fraud. Ramsay reiterated the urgency to prosecute John Gardner Black, who had misled the district by failing to disclose the risk of the investments and by orchestrating a Ponzi scheme that left as many as fifty other school districts and a significant number of municipalities in distress, although no other district's distress could rival ours. I contacted the legislative offices of federal and state leaders like Bud Shuster and Camille "Bud" George. In particular, George advised me as well as all affected superintendents to lobby Harrisburg organizations relentlessly to express our dire financial straits. As George put it well in an April 6, 1998, letter urging superintendents to take concrete political action:

It seems that many of these same organizations are also too preoccupied with monitoring any proposed changes in the school code dealing with investment powers to worry about the schools that are facing disaster.

We met with the Secretary of Education and the Attorney General in the same room on some occasions, all riveted on our mammoth position paper and its undeniable truth. Some of those present disparaged my student letter writing effort as a back-handed attempt to discredit the governor, who showed, at most, some grudging support for our plight. In fact, letters from Treasurer Barbara Hafer and from former governor Dick Thornburgh initially cast blame and responsibility for losses on the ineptitude of our board and administration. When we petitioned the state to apply Act 154 to help us out of the crisis, Hafer flatly responded that "Act 154 was never intended to remedy the past mistakes of school districts." In an AP news release, Thornburgh's stance, while not cozy, at least acknowledged the culpability of other parties:

> Thornburgh told the panel that Black created a pyramid scheme in which he pooled several accounts and used new investors' money to cover his original investors' losses. Mid-State Bank, which handled the accounts, failed to stop him, Thornburgh said.

At one meeting, after braving a chilly, half-hour reception that entailed pointed questions about my tactics, at least one of those across the table articulated that he, too, would do exactly as I had done had he been charged with my circumstances. The Inquisition thawed and we discussed the contents of the report. Governor Ridge had previously assigned special assistant Don Lundy to help us with our case and to assess our financial needs. He expedited our state reimbursements and met with me whenever I visited Harrisburg. Because of Lundy's efforts, we sometimes received our state subsidies in advance to meet our obligations. Meticulous records of cash balances were essential to securing these advances. At my request on November 19, 1997, PSBA's Executive Director Joe Oravitz ran interference for us through the retirement board, on which he had a seat, to see if the board would pick up Devon's bad investments, taking all the huge losses and holding them until maturity so that the funding would not be lost. As former governor Dick Thornburgh had been committed to selling the investments at a loss long before our petition to the retirement board, it did not come as a shock that the board refused. Nonetheless, it was a maneuver we had to explore, in the name of leaving no stone unturned.

The superintendents and business administrators of the other "huge-loss" districts eventually vacated their offices, likely over the ordeal. I could not do so, nor could Cathy Harlow. I could not abdicate my responsibilities to the kids and to the residents of the district—I could never walk away in shame. I knew that I was the political lightning rod for the debacle, and I accepted that. At our lowest point, our spirits could feed on little else but gallows humor, which psychologists name as an apt response to life-changing stress when facing high-cost defeat. We had to laugh along the way to keep our sanity. With dark humor, we drew nautical analogies between the listing district and the Titanic—I the Captain, Cathy Harlow the First-Mate, and all of us attempting to rearrange the deck chairs as the shadows of the iceberg loomed across the bow and the ship descended into the deep waters of the frigid Atlantic.

Still other times our strength was fed by the reassurances of the entire school staff and of the majority of the community—in particular of board member Reverend Norman Huff, who prayed for us regularly. When the critics were howling for board and administrative resignations, a spiritual anchor like Norman was invaluable. We had undergone a hostile school board uprising years earlier, and with Devon it seemed as if the specters of that old coup had rematerialized from the woodwork to haunt us. We were all degraded at public meetings with hundreds of people in attendance, with Joann Lang, my assistant superintendent, so physically ill from the months of abuse years ago that she had to excuse herself from one meeting attended by a throng of critics hungry, perhaps, for revenge. Her Friendship Elementary principal and special education director positions were essentially eliminated under the renegade board of the early 1990's, and these new hostilities affected her in a visceral way. Survival for all of us was a matter of sheer fortitude and character.

Occasionally, I question whether there might have been some way that I (or anyone other than John Black) could have prevented the Devon ordeal. Of that I cannot be sure. At one time I held myself personally responsible. I knew that I was carrying a torch, for I was the finance man and had pushed so stridently for the consolidated building plan. The reality of fraud did not matter at times—I blamed myself, but this only increased my vigor and vigilance to find resolution. I felt the displeasure that emanated from many Tyrone residents and Harrisburg officials and rubbed far too many cold shoulders, including those of State Representative Larry Sather, whose initial icy words I still recall: "Don't try to make your problem my problem." Ultimately, at the behest of Senator Jubelirer and through the voices of informed community members, Sather eventually realized that the Devon crisis was born of fraud, not incompetence. He, too, became an ally.

After innumerable lobbying trips, some fruitful and others unproductive, we ultimately retrieved every cent of lost funding, including most attorney fees. I'm pretty sure that had we not exerted the 24-7 effort needed to achieve our political and fiscal goals during the Devon ordeal that we would not have reclaimed the lost money, for the difference between success and failure is about twenty or more hours beyond the standard forty-hour work-week. I know well the difference between the peak performer and the workaholic, and I am definitely a little of both. The only thing I know for sure is that had I spent the 1997-1999 school years behind my desk, we would never have realized the sweetness of vindication.

I owe so much to so many who aided our just cause, especially Attorney Mike Betts. Mike orchestrated our settlements with third parties like Kutak-Rock and Mid-State Bank, helping all parties avoid going to court, which would have resulted in millions of dollars of litigation and lengthy bouts of grueling public dissatisfaction. Mike knew that the third parties wished to avoid court as much as we did. As Mid-State's settlement agreement of $8,560,927.00 allocated to the district reads:

> The School District and School District Counsel, after taking into account the risks of possible litigation results and the likelihood that this litigation, if not settled now, will be protracted and expensive, are satisfied that the terms and conditions of this Agreement are fair, reasonable, and adequate. This Agreement has been entered into after arm's length negotiations with the Defendants and in good faith . . . The Defendants deny any and all liability to the School District. While denying any and all liability, the Defendants nevertheless recognize that the results of further litigation are uncertain and, should the Action proceed through trial and appeal, substantial and burdensome additional expense would be incurred.

The settlement with Kutak-Rock, reached after two days of intense mediation sessions before the former Chief Judge of the federal district court in Philadelphia, reflected a similar desire to eschew future risk and expense. I was satisfied based upon the negotiations and my discussions with Attorney Betts that the

$4,000,000 settlement offer was the highest recovery we could achieve without very expensive and protracted litigation.

Securing that $4 million was tougher than many might imagine, for Kutak-Rock had offered only $8 million to all of the schools involved in the class-action suit. Counsel for the other schools had tried to swing most of that money away from us, despite the fact that they had ridden our coattails in leading the litigation charge and building the case. That we captured half of that $8 million pool was a huge victory—as was our eventual recovery of 99.4% of the original Devon balances (all of the principal and most of the attorney fees), an outcome virtually unheard of in Ponzi scheme cases. Despite a slew of stress-induced health problems that most likely arose from the ordeal, to this day, a framed copy of the headline from the *Tyrone Daily Herald* hangs in the district's Board Room: *Vindication at Last!*

Cathy and I also felt a great debt to Judge Hiram Carpenter, who acted as a mediator in the process with the third party settlements. He toiled endlessly to secure resolution with Kutak-Rock and Mid-State Bank among others. The school board, former administrators like Neil Smith , and community members like Harry Sickler and so many others were also instrumental. For every Larry Sather slap to the face, there was a Harry Sickler pat on the back—and eventually, as in Sather's case, even the slaps turned into pats—pats from folks like Larrie Derman, Carol Anderson, Jim and Roberta Ramsay, Sam Conrad, and hordes of others too numerous to mention. We needed that emotional support, for many nights when I had reoccurring dreams of someone burning my house down as I struggled to save my dogs. It may be too Freudian to interpret here, but maybe those dogs were the students—I had to put out the financial fire to save them from the consequences. More importantly, I often wonder if our students (without the financial resources to support their programs and instruction) would have achieved the state-leading growth in reading, writing, math, and science that eventually earned them national recognition from organizations and publications like the Education Commission of the States, Standard &Poors, and *U.S. News and World Report*.

Finally, it is consoling to me that we were able to do what our federal government could not even begin to do fifteen years later—prevent the fraud and mismanagement of banks and institutions deemed "too big to fail." Here we were: a small, rural district whose leaders were cast as incompetent rubes who couldn't balance a checkbook. Yet the brightest minds on Wall Street and Goldman-Sachs—some like Hank Paulson, then in leadership positions in the SEC and Federal Reserve—squandered taxpayer money in bailing out the nation's largest banks, not to mention Freddie Mac and Fannie Mae. The entire mortgage-backed securities fiasco that sunk Lehman Brothers and Countrywide and could have easily sunk the nation into another Great Depression was simply Bernie Madoff and Devon Capital Management written exponentially large, with corruption and greed that could have destroyed the nation. The American taxpayer is still paying dearly for the fraud and oversight of others.

Principles of Prevailing

- ✓ Walk around. The high visibility of authority ensures both accountability and productivity.
- ✓ Visit each building regularly to keep a finger on the pulse, speak to all the stakeholders, and understand the complexities of morale.
- ✓ Expect to be blamed as you are an easy target—yet another reason to keep moving.
- ✓ Get to know the power-brokers in the state capital, and do not let their initial coldness deter you.
- ✓ Embrace a spiritual anchor and a sense of humor when the journey gets rough.
- ✓ There is no such thing as a dead end.

"Beware of Greeks bearing gifts."

—Virgil's *Aeneid, II 49.*

3 | Read the Motive

I t's often said that money and power are the dominant motivators for human behavior. However, in an economically depressed area, it often became difficult to recognize monetary motives in the negotiations I undertook on many fronts. Nonetheless, in my tenure as superintendent, I had no sooner become adept at sniffing out the for profit motives of others when I needed to learn how to recognize, understand and address entrenched resistance informed by fear of change, although the response was often couched within an ideological motive. This lesson tells the story of how I learned to read the motive before I could address the problem.

In the late 1990's, in addition to renovating the high school, the board decided to consolidate all of our elementary schools into one new building beside the high school. This decision was predicated on these interactive factors: 1) educational inequality among the schools 2) dire building conditions and 3) predicted population growth flat or in decline. Many of those in the rural stretches of our district opposed sending their children to school "in town," as they would be removed from their family cultures for longer periods of time at an early age. Nonetheless, the board was interested in purchasing about thirty-five acres of the property adjacent to the planned school. Initially deliberating with the borough manager, we received the demand that we widen the access roads to the adjacent property, lay down sidewalks to meet code, and pave the entire area of Clay Avenue and 5th Street that would lead to the parcel. At the time, the estimated cost of the paving work was around $400,000, which would not be reimbursable from the state—unlike the state aid-ratio reimbursement we received for the construction of the actual school buildings and for the actual site. The wrinkle, of course, was the $400,000 required by the borough manager—not to mention all the additional and unforeseen costs, including the hiring of an architect, which might have pushed the total cost closer to $500,000.

Enter Frank, bearing gifts. One would not expect Trump University-style real estate tactics to be employed by an ordinary farmer in a rural part of our district. But then again, though a local, Frank was no ordinary farmer. As much a real estate developer and "ad-venture" capitalist as he was a farmer, Frank was a formidable businessman whose rightful goal was to make a profit.

Smelling our dilemma, and his potential gain as a result, Frank attempted to give the school district a parcel of land in a rural area so that we could build an elementary school there, as well as the one in town where students of more diverse academic, socio-economic, and behavioral backgrounds would attend. Some may speculate that if Frank succeeded, not only would he profit immeasurably by the soaring value of his own real estate holdings with a neighborhood school nearby, but he would also be something of a champion in the eyes of rural opponents to the district's consolidation plan. Alas, the existing neighborhood school might perish, but another would rise from its ashes, preserving the relative homogeneity of rural classrooms.

Many residents envisioned imminent population growth in both the rural areas nearer State College and in the Tyrone areas, a product of the completion of the Interstate 99 corridor connecting Altoona and State College—the culmination of industry-building efforts spearheaded by capital-raising entities like the Altoona Blair County Development Corporation. With infrastructure and employment opportunity like this at the door, folks assumed that the district's population had no choice but to swell. But the growth never occurred. In fact, student population in every Blair and Huntingdon County district dwindled over the ensuing decade—in keeping with the state-wide trend. As it turned out, the much-ballyhooed Tyrone By-pass of Interstate 99 was just that—a faster way to bypass Tyrone.

Not to be discouraged, Frank pursued the purchase of the thirty-five acres from underneath the district. Perhaps he knew that we had to seek approval for reimbursement for the land with the state and that this process would demand more time than it would for him (as an individual) to purchase the property. So Frank engineered a discussion with the owners. He predicated his proposed purchase on the premise that he would build a housing development on that acreage.

I talked directly with the owners regarding Frank's contact, especially to address the reality that we had to slow down the process so we could hear back from the state regarding the reimbursement, which amounted to roughly 70% of the purchase price of $247,000. Without delay, Business Administrator Cathy Harlow joined me to meet Frank and his wife to broker a deal over coffee at his home.

I was brusque: "What do you want to make a deal for the land? If the district is buying it from you, how much profit do you want to make?" Reluctant to respond, or perhaps burdened with second thoughts, Frank's motive remained, to me, rather clear: he owned all of the lands immediately surrounding the plot that he was planning to "give" us. The surrounding acreage, when and if he planned to sell it, would be extremely lucrative.

So discussions with the board progressed, eventually leading us to use what were at that time the girls' softball 'and the boys' baseball fields to build the new elementary complex: a three-level structure which students and staff would enter on the second level. At this time, we had to get township approval for police authority on Clay Avenue because of the increased traffic. One Snyder Township Supervisor was not the easiest gentleman with whom to deal—he was solidly against the construction, though we made it clear that we did not need township approval to pursue it. Ultimately, the township granted approval for the school to use school patrols to direct traffic without authority to enforce laws and issue fines as provided by Pennsylvania's school code; he gave the district a lot of grief, but not nearly as much as Barb and Judy, who clearly defined their position on this matter in this strategic advertisement entitled "WHY?" in the *Tyrone Daily Herald:*

> **WHY** when at a January 1997 board meeting, the question was asked, "What is the current cost of the building project?" was the answer: "We do not know."
>
> **WHY** when a local farm was for sale—200 acres at $200,000 [sic] did our Superintendent purchase 35 acres for $247,000? Did any board members attend these meetings? No. Now is the time to replace these people who have allowed the Superintendent to put

us so far in debt that most of us or maybe all of us will never see the debt paid. You have allowed the administration and school board to close good neighborhood schools.

WHY when the above land was purchased by another individual, did only our Superintendent and Business Administrator negotiate to re-purchase this land? No Board Members attend[ed] these meetings.

WHY when trying to get approval from the Snyder Township Supervisors did our Superintendent, architect and school attorney attend meetings—but no school board members were present?

REMEMBER, TUESDAY, MAY 20 IS ELECTION DAY. VOTE FOR THE PEOPLE WHO ARE INTERESTED IN THE EDUCATION OF THEIR CHILDREN AS WELL AS YOURS. WE ARE NOT IN THE BUSINESS OF BRICKS AND MORTAR—BUT IN THE BUSINESS OF EDUCATION.

VOTE FOR [JUDY] AND [BARB], SCHOOL DIRECTORS

On one point Judy and Barb were correct: school boards and superintendents should not be in the business of bricks and mortar, but in the education of kids. Yet the truth is that the sternest opponents of school consolidation, many of whom yearned for a version of Garrison Keillor's Lake Woebegone ("where all the women are strong, all the men are good-looking, and all the kids are above average") were not necessarily invested in the "education of their children as well as yours." Such investment was the ultimate goal of consolidation: to educate all kids equally. Motivated not by equal access to quality education , many folks were instead motivated by fear—a fear that they would lose their kids in an impersonal, monolithic building further away from their homes; that the newfangled, impersonal school would not reflect their values; that the educational rigor that they experienced at their quaint, old school would be lost.

The real fear was certainly not insurmountable debt, as Judy and Barb alleged. In fact, in August of 2013 (the year that I retired), the board retired the debt on the consolidated building projects—just as my father Norman Miller in 1971 had made as one of his final acts as superintendent to retire all construction debts incurred during his tenure. What did *not* retire is a record of explosive educational growth, with students from Tyrone Area High School—students who were kindergarteners in the nascent years of the consolidated elementary school—graduating high school thirteen years later with composite value-added scores PVAAS (Pennsylvania value added assessment system) in reading, writing, math, and science at the very top of the state, competing not just alongside but ahead of the most prestigious school districts Pennsylvania tax dollars could fund. The 2012 graphic below tells the tale:

State Rank	2012 11th Grade PSSA Results for Reading, Writing, Math, and Science	Value Added
1	*Tyrone Area School District*	*534*
2	Portage Area School District	361
3	Rose Tree Media School District	347
4	Sharpsville Area School District	333
5	Hampton Township School District	302
6	Windber Area School District	296
7	Tredyffrin-Easttown School District	290
8	Mt Lebanon School District	281
9	Springfield Township School District	275
10	Wallingford-Swarthmore School District	269

Source: https://pvaas.sas.com. November 20, 2012.

Much earlier, during the early 1980s when a team of teachers and administrators fought to initiate full-day kindergarten in Tyrone, it had also been critical for me to unearth and to understand the fear of change as a fundamental political motive for parents of students in our school district. The only schools near us with full-day kindergarten at that time were Lock Haven and Homer Center—both around sixty miles away. Our staff researched the full-day kindergarten model fully by visiting Homer Center and other sites that had successfully implemented it for three years, returning impressed with their findings. Four Kindergarten teachers with Curriculum Supervisor Bill Baker, reading specialist Carol Blundell, and nationally-acclaimed Early

Childhood Advocate Theo Spewock, all presented their findings to the board, along with a panel of principals including Brad Aults and John Vendetti as well as teachers Karen Raffeto, Jean Parker, Anna Myers, and Joline Hannold. Spewock's preschool program was voted best in the state in 1992, so our proposal and research boasted significant authority. If we would adopt full-day kindergarten in our district, more time could be afforded for formal and creative academics, social interaction, and certainly greater readiness for first grade literacy. In addition to mounds of empirical statistical data bolstering these claims, a Homer Center parent whose first-grade child had experienced the program reported anecdotally that, because of his exposure to the Homer Center program, her child was far ahead of the rest of her first-grade class when she moved to Tyrone

Imagine our initial bewilderment, then, when, even after that bundle of research and anecdotal evidence supportive of full-day kindergarten, hundreds of parents attended public meetings designed to contest this issue. Many of those present were not prepared for the change and could not accept it. Even Dr. Daniel Friday, noted obstetrician, spoke openly in opposition to full-day kindergarten and received a round of applause. Parents' pretexts were certainly not fiscal; there was sufficient money to cover the hiring of teachers to implement full-day education. In fact, additional state reimbursements based on WADM's (weighted average daily membership) combined with the elimination of noon-time transportation costs produced a program that virtually paid for itself. Instead of monetary concerns, this was the list of objections enumerated in the April 1, 1981 edition of the *Tyrone Daily Herald*:

1. The school day is too long for a 5-year old. Some bused children would be gone from 7 AM to 4 PM.
2. They would be exposed to older children too long, not only at school but on the bus—they'd be intimidated.
3. They could catch colds or illness from taking naps on cots in school rather than in beds at home. Children do not rest well with other children around.
4. Too much academics too soon.
5. They are taken away from the family too soon.
6. Rural children possibly having to change buses at the high school may experience confusion and fright.
7. If the plan saves money—there's no reason to save it by making the children suffer.
8. Will the full-day program become all-day babysitting?

9. Kindergarten should be a learning experience where children are slowly introduced to school.
10. The cafeteria experience (using and carrying money they don't know about, carrying trays, short eating time) may cause some confusion.

While most objectors were sincerely afraid, others saw the curriculum move as nothing more than a money-saving ploy. As concerned citizen Ben speculated in an April 10 letter to the editor, the push for full-day kindergarten smelled of conspiracy and shady card-dealing:

> Folks, I think it's time to put the cards on the table and call it as I see it. ALL DAY KINDERGARTEN IS BUNK!
>
> And who's kidding who—if all this is just rumors, then why has the librarian at the Adams School been told to move her library to the basement for the coming school year to make room for the new kindergarten class?
>
> I just feel it's another ploy to lull us to sleep, and then . . . POW! It's too late, because the superintendent recommended it, the school board passed it, and the deed is done . . .
>
> If there is any good reason for the change other than to get more money for the school system merely on an all-day attendance count, I think that stinks.

With such vehement opposition expressed at each board meeting, when it came down to the final vote, I whispered these words to President Hickes when he looked at me in dismay: "Let a board member make a motion, get a second, and then vote to turn it down." My strategy was to let the administration take the hit. So we cut the noontime kindergarten transportation and accumulated the money for a future implementation date. We'd revisit the issue later. Part of everything in life is timing—when to act promptly and when to prepare for another day.

The grand irony, of course, is that in another year or two we offered one or two pilot classes of full-day kindergarten at parents' request. The requests eventually blossomed into a waiting list during the ensuing year, waiting lists that became so unwieldy that we fully implemented the program by virtue of sheer public demand. This is precisely what happens at times when a school acts proactively. Now, full-day programs are the national norm. The lessons that I distilled from the incident were that as an administrator I needed to develop patience and to understand when resistance to change is based on fear. Fear is one of the most powerful drivers of personal and political motive; it even guides our economic and spiritual lives to a great extent. Patience sometimes is the only viable political answer to fear—the type of patience that says, "Hey, I hear you, but you wait—you'll change your mind . . . just watch." So the pilot program that we initiated at the request of less fearful parents allowed more fearful parents to watch. And behold, they liked what they saw. It is no easy task to restrain a program whose time has come. However, ramrodding a new program without broad public backing has dire political consequences, while patience will always allow an excellent program to materialize.

What materialized after both the elementary school consolidation of the 1990's and all-day kindergarten in the early 1980's kicked in was Theo Spewock's pre-school literacy program, that at one point ranked tops in the state. What dissipated were the stubborn achievement gaps that once plagued neighborhood schools like Madison, literally entrenched on what many perceived as "the wrong side of the tracks" that ran through town, while Elizabethtown and Friendship harbored what many perceived as the academic elite.

In Tyrone, thanks in large measure to consolidation, poor students now learn alongside wealthier ones; kids with learning challenges sit in the same classrooms as those with learning gifts. And the greatest gift they all enjoy is a fair shot at the future.

Principles of Prevailing

- ✓ People are obviously motivated by money. Instead of begrudging them, ask what you can get from them in exchange.
- ✓ People will use the welfare of school kids to cloak ulterior motives—monetary or otherwise.
- ✓ Unlike obvious motives like money, fear goes largely unrecognized; only after understanding a person's fear (especially the fear of change) can you begin to change minds to shape effective programs and policies.

> *"Power is no blessing in itself, except when it is used to protect the innocent."*
>
> —Jonathan Swift

4 | Protect the Kids

For centuries, the sexual abuse of children has stained those institutions, from home and church to schools and colleges that are ostensibly designed to nurture and protect the young. Many cultures, until recently, have normalized the sexual abuse of children by adults as a kind of rite of passage. The ancient Greeks condoned the sexual exploitation of youth—especially in educational settings. As removed and repugnant as this practice is from the twenty-first century vantage point, it resonates in the wake of the 2011 Penn State sexual abuse scandal, which revealed the fiasco which occurred when officials failed to respond properly to that horrific situation. Purportedly, the ancient Greeks espoused such abuse in order to inculcate moral and cultural values, while elsewhere in antiquity the Romans were far less "civic-minded" in their exploitation, with men commonly using their status to extract sexual favors from social inferiors, especially kids.

The stark reality is that predators are always on the groom; they prowl America's streets, churches, and hallways every day with hawk-like sensitivity to the intellectual, physical, emotional, or social vulnerabilities that young folks harbor. Those who protect them from justice for the sake of political or fiscal solvency commit an equally abhorrent evil and blur the moral line until it is not clear which is more important—the success of the school or the innocence of the child. It is hard for most folks to fathom how no initial action was taken on behalf of Penn State against Sandusky more severe than having his key confiscated, restricting but not eliminating his access to campus facilities. According to investigator Louis Freeh, even after Penn State authorities were made aware of Sandusky's exploits, no report was made to police or to a child protection agency—a breach of state law. As I recall my own initial experience with abuse many decades ago through the more recent layers of the Sandusky/Penn State incident, it underscores how easy it is for modern as well as ancient societies to find a way to ignore if not condone sexual abuse.

The U.S.'s late twentieth and early twenty-first century culture seem steeped in awareness on all levels of child sexual abuse as a federal, actionable crime. However, my first official intervention in protecting our students from a sexual predator occurred on the very cusp of those new laws and of a widespread cultural shift in awareness about sexual abuse. In fact, my second year as superintendent, 1972-1973, coincided with Congressional hearings that eventually rendered child sexual abuse a violation of federal and state law; it also marked my first lesson in the necessity of a swift response to charges of inappropriate teacher interactions with students.

As the current principal was experiencing a rash of time-consuming pressures at that point, I involved myself in a reported case of teacher-student sexual activity at the earliest possible stage. It was reported to me that the teacher housed a projector with which he showed pornographic films to his female students in a storage closet behind his room. Also rumored—but not officially reported—were lurid tales of sexual contact with female students. These tales seemed fully within character in light of earlier rumors that this teacher had at least on one occasion invited students to his home for parties and offered them wine. I had approached him about this party a good year prior to these freshest charges, so without hesitation, I scouted out the teacher's lair early in the morning, placed the films I found there into his projector, and corroborated the reports of on-campus pornography.

At that time there were no Weingarten rights[3] guaranteeing the teacher a spokesperson from the union, so I escorted him to the principal's suite and talked freely about his rumored sexual exploits involving female high school students. Upon serious questioning from me, he admitted that he had engaged in sexual relations with several girls, after which I left the room and called the county district attorney for advice on how to handle the case. I then gave the teacher in question the option of either resigning immediately or facing the labyrinthine channels of the court system, after which we would dismiss him from employment anyway. He contacted his lawyer, who called me and asked for a letter of recommendation for the teacher as a prerequisite for his resignation—and as a license, I suppose, to prey on young girls elsewhere. I refused to give him a letter of recommendation, so he and his wife exited the district very quickly.

But the most shocking and, at that time, confusing part of this story did not end here. It was this: many of the students at the time felt a fierce loyalty to this teacher, seemingly oblivious to the abuse of power and the abdication of professional responsibility his behavior with female students indicated. Of course, word of our personnel action circulated rapidly, as I also called in another qualified teacher to take over. Within several days it was rumored that, in protest of the previous teacher's termination, the students would not perform under the direction of a new teacher at a scheduled public performance. Many of these students claimed that the purported victims had made the decision by themselves to engage in sexual relations with their teacher and that his intimate encounters were "all right with them." They wholeheartedly supported the abuser. I even received a call from one of my former students exhorting me to drop all action against the director, although he had by then resigned.

With the historical perspective I try to bring to much of my administrative understanding and decision-making, the student reaction to Case 1's dismissal now makes sense through a number of lenses. For one, the teacher's sexual misconduct took place in the midst of the sexual counter-culture of the early

---

3 Weingarten rights guarantee an employee the right to Union representation during an investigatory interview. These rights, established by the Supreme Court, in 1975 in the case of J'. Weingarten Inc., must be claimed by the employee. The supervisor has no obligation to inform an employee that s/he is entitled to Union representation.
Source http://definitions.uslegal.com/w/weingarten-rights/

seventies. After all, even many of our rural kids were immersed in the purple haze of free-love music, and the fumes from Woodstock still lingered in the air. Furthermore, there was at that time minimal media exposure to teacher misconduct and little to no public naming of adult sexual behavior with minors as an illegal and damaging abuse of power. What we now know in light of the last thirty years' abuse discourse focuses on the enmeshed psychological dynamic and blurred boundaries between abuser and victim. Many of us have been educated over the decades following the 1970's about how victims often protect abusers, sexual and otherwise, out of a sense of what they name as the love and special treatment shown to them, often by an elder to a vulnerable child or teenager. In part, that dynamic explains the students' loyalty after the teacher was dismissed from the district. Finally, the early seventies predated the explosion of electronic communication. Today, when teachers nationwide engage in affairs with students, rumors swirl about predatory teachers. Students tweet about it in real time. Outraged parents network to distribute action plans. Schools dispatch counselors to assuage the pain.

More specific historicizing and hindsight also give us a comparative perspective on the incident that appeared singular and puzzling to me at the time. One has only to look at the infamous cases of sexual exploitation at the highly regarded Horace Mann[4] preparatory school in the late 1970's to see illustrated victim loyalty and love of an adult abuser. People don't understand," one of the Horace Mann victims told *New Yorker* columnist Marc Fisher decades later. "People think of child abuse as a moment in a shower, like Sandusky. They don't think of it as essentially abducting and brainwashing. This was a cult of art, literature, and music, a cult that was revered in some circles." Fischer reports that many of the Horace Mann victims wanted their abusers to be held accountable—and yet one in particular, a boy named Gene, still holds on to a statuette given to him by his abuser in the grooming process: "This [statuette] meant that somebody loved me, and nobody had ever shown me that before," Gene says. "It's a conundrum. Why don't I just drop it in the garbage right now? It's part of me, part of my life. I guess I'll be done with it when I don't need somebody's love." The student pointed out that his abuser counted on everyone's silence. I am

---

4 An independent Pre-Kindergarten through 12th grade establishment in the Riverdale neighborhood of the Bronx. In the late 1970's over 60 cases of sexual assault were reported. In 2015, more sexual assault cases were reported. Source http://www.refinery29.com/2015/05/88146/horace-mann-sexual-abuse-update

sure it was so with Case 1's Tyrone victims—that he assumed that his students' humiliation, his promises to them, and their misguided loyalty would keep them quiet as he preyed on their need for affirmation.

I often think that those protesting students carrying Case 1's banner may have felt differently had they pursued the opportunity to talk sincerely and deeply with his victims—either near the time of the abuse or decades later—about their contacts with him, about how he undoubtedly groomed them and exploited them with favors and self-serving compliments. I doubt that those protestors would have perceived him any longer as an innocent participant in consensual relationships—especially years hence as adults, with their own daughters in his classroom. Nonetheless, while student reaction to the teacher's exit were, perhaps, dazed and confused by the early 70's sexual revolution and anti-war rebellion, I was very clear at the time about the politics, ethics and necessity of my immediate intervention in Case 1's inappropriate and illegal misconduct with students. Time has only confirmed the rightness of that resolve.

The politics were not, however, so clear in the situation of Case 2, as it involved two consensual adults in a situation in which neither broke a law nor violated a professional responsibility. While this case did not involve the abuse of a child, I mention it here because it did involve enough sexual intrigue to cause significant disruption to the school and its operation and reputation—especially if it were allowed to become a Jerry Springer-style media circus. Thus, a failure to address it might have had political repercussion in a highly conservative small-town community like Tyrone, where the odor of dirty laundry can intensify and travel quickly.

The teacher, who had been married for decades, became sympathetic to a woman's marital difficulties, and before long their counseling relationship blossomed into a sexual one. At the beginning of the school year in the early 70's, the woman marched into one of our schools declaring that the teacher was the father of her recently born child and demanding that he provide child support. The scene transpired at the opening day in-service training session, so teachers in that building were present for the side-show. I quickly corralled the couple, separated them, and clarified that their crisis was "between the two of them." I offered to help them, with the contingency that the sexual relationship and its aftermath must not be made a public issue. The female teacher agreed, and I said that I would certainly support her in her cause and exhort the male teacher to pay child support, although he was resistant to the idea. I persuaded him that if their disagreement went public, which it could at any time, I was not certain what the board's response would be. I put the teacher in the position that if he and the woman involved continued to make a public spectacle over this issue, that they could both lose their jobs. After speaking with him on a number of occasions regarding the serious repercussions that he might face, the teacher finally came on board with the prospect of paying child support. Of course, the most vital outcome in this case was that the teacher had consented to provide for his child, but a corollary result for the district of my taking this situation on privately, was squelching a potential media or political flare-up on the part of a conservative board and community.

Obviously, the potential for political flare-ups is amplified when on-campus sex between teachers and students are involved, as in Case 1. Yet the potential for political damage is still enormous whenever teachers engage in improprieties off-campus—even when those involved are from outside the school district. Those were the circumstances with Case 3. In 1986, a male teacher from our district was involved in sexual behaviors with males of undisclosed ages at the Station Mall in neighboring Altoona, Pennsylvania. An undercover police operation over a three-week period in the restrooms at the mall revealed the indiscretions. The activity was reported by the *Altoona Mirror*, and, of course, the identities of all adult individuals involved—including those of other employees from other school districts as well as the employee from ours—were detailed.

The incendiary potential for our district around this sexual scandal was greater than the earlier incidences that I have described because this one involved same-sex sexual contact in an ultra-conservative community prior to more recent LGBT visibility and enfranchisement. This explains the reaction of one of several members of the board who demanded that we have a board hearing over the indiscretions on the part of the teacher and take action, thereby showering further public humiliation on the teacher. It may be noted that since this school board member had long harbored a vendetta against me, he may well have hoped, by process of association, to also humiliate our school district's administration during these public hearings. I disagreed with this approach and worked with Case 3 and Bill Mingle, the Teacher Association's representative, on delineating the terms of the teacher's termination. Secure in the knowledge that the teacher faced criminal charges that would preclude his future employment anywhere. The board agreed to the terms that the teacher be paid for his accumulated sick days, dodging further public humiliation for both him and the school district. Our action was similar to the action taken by other districts such as Hollidaysburg and Altoona, who also disciplined teachers involved in the same Station Mall morals corruption sting. Case 3 was accepted into an accelerated rehabilitation disposition and his resignation was executed.

The final incident I would like to illustrate in which I was called upon to protect the kids involves a much more disputable cluster of claims; my steps to solve the problem therefore placed me and the district in a more nebulous posture both legally and ethically. Case 4 involved a popular teacher whose conflicted personal values about sex clashed with the attempts of our school board to instill both ethical values and contraceptive knowledge in our student population. It must be stated that the teacher was never accused of having sexual relations with any minor either inside or outside the district. However, although married and a parent, Case 4 practiced open marriage habits in a small, conservative community that at least publically espoused that marriage vows should limit the number of one's sexual partners. Thus, Case 4's repeated public indiscretions and lapses of good judgment eventually led to some unfortunate consequences. Although he may never have behaved in an untoward way to any of our students , his public persona prejudiced enough board members, parents, and students against him that the loss of all moral credibility caused further professional disaster for him and complications for district policy about protecting our students.

While married, Case 4 had an extramarital child with a paramour. When I confronted Case 4 with the gossip that had emerged from the affair, the individual gave me the story that the lover put on forceful sexual advances. As a result of this incident, Case 4's wages eventually were garnished for child support. I had met with Case 4 about the effect of this indiscretion on ethical and professional credibility and on relationships with students. Certain board members agreed to remove Case 4 from extracurricular positions at the time. However, during this process I received a visit from an acquaintance of Case 4 in my office, whose intimidating message to me was that I should not move forward with any action against this teacher. Using my most discrete manner possible in interacting with this visitor, I moved forward to limit the teacher's reach with the knowledge that Case 4's indiscretions were impossible for us as an administration and board to defend if we acted in the best interest of the community.

Despite all of our attempts to counsel Case 4, given his loss of moral credibility, he became a casualty of his own indiscretions as much as of student perceptions of his moral laxness. The climactic incident transpired with female middle-school students who were purportedly being touched inappropriately by this teacher. This activity was initially reported by male students in Case 4's classes. The girls, it must be noted, never reported any abuse—only the boys, who had witnessed the teacher's behavior and found it troubling enough to report to their parents. All reported cases of touching were fully public—occurring in the context of a class game.

I met with some parents of both the male and the female students both individually and together so that I could explain to them how I planned to address their teacher's behaviors and the accusations surrounding them. Case 4 never hired an attorney in either of these situations, nor did the teacher admit to touching female students in an inappropriate manner. Even at my recommendation, the teacher declined union representation. In fact, the teacher argued that any touching was incidental if it occurred at all. The defense was that Case 4 was attempting to teach students how to hold and pass a ball between their legs. It was reported that at least one girl, however, accused Case 4 of putting hands on her shoulders in a class activity—again publicly. Case 4 claimed this action was an attempt to console her. We had worked toward a resignation, which we did not receive. Eventually, perhaps imagining the prospect of legal action that parents might pursue, the teacher chose instead to retire, as he was nearing retirement age anyway. No parents pursued legal recourse, nor did we, upon the recommendation of school counsel Cynthia Yeager, thus sparing the young girls the trauma of a hearing. The goal was accomplished: Case 4 was no longer a potential threat to kids. Like the teacher in Case 1 of decades earlier, Case 4 asked for a letter of recommendation. Instead, the letter included only Case 4's date of hire and date of retirement; that was all.

Over the years, I encountered close to forty cases of alleged faculty-staff sexual misconduct involving varying degrees of severity. My method of dealing with these was always to point out options for those support staff and teachers involved. In all cases of sexual indiscretion—whether with students or with other teachers, with minors or with adults, on-campus or off-campus, within the law or outside the law—I applied both an ethical and a political constant: protect kids first, and then act to ensure the moral and institutional credibility of the district.

The order of that sequence is paramount. When political motive dislodges the ethical imperative, as it appears to have from the Catholic Church to the Penn State abuse scandals, then no child is safe—nor is the institution in charge.

Principles of Prevailing

- ✓ Those who protect predators from justice for the sake of political or fiscal solvency commit an equally abhorrent evil.
- ✓ Make a swift response to charges of inappropriate interactions with students.
- ✓ Against all logic, kids may defend those who exploit them; do not rest until the exploiter, however popular, is removed.
- ✓ A failure to address sexual indiscretions among staff on or off campus may have political repercussions in a highly conservative community. Do not hesitate to counsel or to recommend counseling for the staff members involved and to recommend a course of action.
- ✓ Protect kids first, and then the district

"Life really wouldn't be worth livin' if you didn't have a high school football team to support."

—H.G. Bissinger
Odessa, Texas realtor Bob Rutherford in *Friday Night Lights*

5 | Know Your ABC's
Athletics, Band, & Chorus

The *New York Times* said this about H. G. Bissinger's true-life account of the Permian Panther football community in his wildly popular book *Friday Night Lights*: "[This work] offers a biting indictment of the sports craziness that . . . grips most of American society, while at the same time providing a moving evocation of its powerful allure."

It is not much of an imaginative leap to travel from Odessa, Texas to Tyrone, Pennsylvania. Although football dominates our town's cultural landscape and values, Tyrone school boards under my tenure have always supported diverse areas of student endeavor, understanding and engaging the spirited small-town ethos behind successes in sports as well as in the arts and academics. In fact, to Tyrone's credit, in 2011 the high school scored the equivalent of a Triple Crown in Pennsylvania. Among 542 Pennsylvania public schools, cyber schools, and charter schools, the Golden Eagles ranked first in all three endeavors. In music, the competitive marching band finished first in class 2A with an 88.3 performance at the Atlantic Coast Championships. In the classroom, students scored the state's highest value-added academic growth in all four tested subjects combined for the first of two consecutive years, recording 541.4 scaled score points above expectation. And in football, the team ended its season as the top-ranked public school unit in the state in class AA. Only Lancaster Catholic, a much larger parochial school, finished ahead of the Golden Eagles. It may not have been the case in Odessa under the evocative grip of their Texas-style football lights, but under the glow of Tyrone's lights one thing was always clear to me, if not to all of Tyrone's football fans: the students wearing black and orange were just that—students. While virtually all school board members over the years publically agreed with that notion, occasionally one might act from another playbook.

At those times, the politics became foul.

My father, who preceded me as superintendent of Tyrone's schools, frequently offered this bit of wisdom when I was growing up: "It's always best when the football team goes 8-2." It seemed like such an arbitrary number to me back then, if not a defeatist one at that.

Why not go undefeated?

But after working in the school system for five decades and watching the powerful allure that both undefeated and winless seasons had on the pulse of political and financial maneuverings, especially with regard to coaching personnel, I now get my father's meaning.

Ranked seventeenth all-time in Pennsylvania football history, Tyrone has recorded nearly 650 victories. Until 2014, Tyrone boasted the only team in District 6 at any size classification to have achieved the holy grail of a state championship—a distinction it now shares with single-A champion Bishop Guilfoyle.

However, before John Franco assumed command of the Golden Eagle football team, the program had endured a humiliating string of losing seasons unlike any other in its storied history. It all started with a forlorn 1-9 campaign under a previously successful coach who had experienced mounting difficulties in the classroom and had to be relieved of his duties. The remedy was to hire an ex-NFL player who many believed would whip the Eagles into shape. The NFL retiree finished 2-8, in large measure because he believed in cancelling Monday practices and had no intentions of logging more hours than were absolutely necessary for him to collect a stipend. Despite numerous coaching changes, four coaches within one four-year stretch had accrued cumulative damages set at 4-35. We recruited former coaches who had experienced modest successes with above .500 or near .500 slates, but the results were not gratifying to many.

Enter John Franco, a driver education instructor at Altoona High School who became disenchanted with the lack of support he received as head coach there. His record at Altoona was tepid at best, and in Franco's first year at Tyrone, he commanded an equally unimpressive .500 record. Amid a winter of gridiron discontent, however, tepid and average were enough to inspire both the players and the community. In Franco's second season, though, his team advanced to the state AA final-four. Over his full tenure at Tyrone, he and his players ultimately broke nearly every record on the books, finishing his Tyrone career at 190-37, an unparalleled .837 winning percentage, with a 1999 state title, two-time PA Coach of the Year honors, and numerous district titles. Only Steve Jacobs with 100 wins from the 1940's and 1950's came close to Franco's success.

Given all of this, it is little wonder that in 2012 a controversy emerged surrounding John Franco's personal decision to leave Tyrone as football coach and return to his native Altoona when presented with a new coaching opportunity there. Franco's motives should have been clear enough to any Tyrone Football booster—his sons had graduated from Tyrone by 2011 with football success notable enough to land them scholarships with NCAA Division 1 college squads at Army and Akron, even though both eventually transferred to Division II Indiana University of Pennsylvania. While coaching at Tyrone, Franco lived in town to be close to the team, but he taught at Altoona, so he had to commute daily to work. Once his sons had graduated from our high school, it was natural for him to sell his Tyrone residence and move back to Altoona to both work and live.

One can understand if not applaud the efforts of many Tyrone boosters, parents, and students to keep Coach Franco in Tyrone—in essence, to "buy him back" by creating a lucrative, comfortable position in our district. Problematically, however, all Pennsylvania schools in 2011 were plagued by a period of radical economic efficiency because of skyrocketing pension costs and monumental budget cuts by the Corbett administration. In an era of "do more with less," we had little to do much with at all. In fact, we had terminated several programs and teaching positions through attrition that year because of a million dollar plunge in state funding. How could we create a cozy position for a football coach after we had just slashed academic and vocational programs—and when further cuts would be on the horizon? How could we justify special dispensations to an extracurricular activity whenever both of our educational support and teacher contracts were soon to be negotiated—and when those contracts would ask staff to expect less and work more? Offering Coach Franco a sweet deal would create the fundamental problem of unfairness, especially to staff members like paraprofessionals, who made only $8 or $9 per hour. How could we justify our school's mission to them and to the kids that they worked so hard to help when programs, resources, hours, and benefits were being slashed to finance a luxury job for a football coach? Hiring Franco as an athletic director as he requested was simply not feasible, since our current director was receiving only a small stipend while teaching physical education half-time. It would be unfair and unjust to remove our current director to afford John that opportunity. Perhaps John was unaware of the nature of the current athletic director position, and of the fiscal pressure his request was placing on our district.

It was political dynamite as well as an unjustifiable divergence from our mission and values for us to negotiate with Franco as he considered counter-offers from Altoona simultaneously. There was a bit of strategy here from Altoona regarding potential changes in his schedule as well. He had been a driver education teacher for many years, and now Altoona was thinking about nudging him into a physical education slot. After John had taught driver's education for decades, a possible schedule change would occur that would force him into relatively unfamiliar ground. It was about this time when the Tyrone board became more involved, hoping to sway John's loyalties back to Tyrone, where a position much more attractive might be crafted. I became involved too at this point—especially when eighty people showed up at a board meeting with this as the banner: "Whatever John Franco wants, John Franco should get [as shared by at least one citizen], even if that is the superintendent's salary!" When individuals within any organization experience a great degree of success, they tend to aggregate such loyal followings. But the question remained: is this an athletic school or an academic one? I was convinced that as we had essentially starved the Academic Beast in the latest budget, we simply could not justify turning around to feed the Athletic Beast its lunch. Although many of our townspeople valued our football team's identity and success above most things, the board and the administration continued to see the district as academics first and athletics second, acknowledging that the two spheres formed a unified whole.

During several negotiations with John Franco, his proposal suggested a position of $60,000 as an athletic director or a dean of some kind. In essence, what he asked for in order to stay in Tyrone was for us to create a position just for him—a job that with benefits would have run over $80,000, not including his football stipend, which would stretch him further toward the $90,000 range. The only counter offer that we made was a significant and unanimously approved increase in his extra-curricular fee for coaching football from $6,858.43 to $11,000.00.

As the board and I discussed, "How can we consider potential cuts in teaching staff and other staff and still consider giving Franco what he wants?" Granted, he did a great job as a football coach and had been a very important part of the lives of those who played for him. In fact, John and his wife had often conducted on their own time tutoring sessions for athletes on the cusp of failure and academic eligibility. I am sure this is much more than what the fire-breathing Texas coaches like Randy Mayes in *Friday Night Lights* do for their athletes in those gridiron-crazy towns with college-capacity stadiums, artificial-turf and coaching-only positions approaching or eclipsing a hundred grand a year. Nonetheless, we had to decide what was most important for all students—and that was to maintain as many qualified teachers as possible. Besides, the reality was that we had no positions available for John, especially since he lacked other certifications other than health/physical education and driver's education. We currently had two teachers with driver's education papers—how could we justify another? On top of this, we had already slashed our driver's education program, eliminating in-school classroom driver classes to better utilize staff in core subjects. Students had been paying a $50 fee to take driver education behind-the-wheel instruction after school hours and free after-school classroom courses paid by the district. Of these cost-reducing measures that further compromised any offer we would make to Franco, I am pretty sure John's supporters were unaware.

So Altoona essentially had Franco—and they were threatening him in a way, suggesting that if he did not take their head coaching position that they would relegate him to teaching gym, which he likely wanted to avoid. So Coach Franco—not the Tyrone Area School Board—made the decision to move. He certainly had the opportunity to remain at Tyrone—and at a significantly higher coaching salary than what he had earned for the previous season. Eschewing the physical education assignment and embracing what might have amounted to higher pension calculations for his future, he opted to take the head coaching job at Altoona.

Despite the financial and professional implications for John Franco, the majority of the Tyrone board was content with the manner in which the Franco case was handled, foremost because our move was supportive of our students and sensitive to our staff. Having endured two challenging seasons with the Altoona Mountain Lions in 2012 and 2013 when rabid fans were demanding winning campaigns, perhaps John Franco wished that he had never left Tyrone. He may have learned that his successes at our school had as much to do with our faith in him as it did with what he had to offer our kids. As it turned out in the winter of 2014, local papers reported that Franco might be attempting to return to Tyrone. Current coach Steve Guthoff resigned shortly after these reports surfaced, purportedly to open the door for John should he wish to return as head coach. One of Franco's former players at Tyrone promptly gathered a petition of over 500 signatures to convince the board to court Franco, but some Altoona residents found fault with what they perceived to be greed on John's part. As Altoona resident Mike Gibbons oversimplified the matter with the *Altoona Mirror* editor—perhaps a bit wildly and unfairly:

> Please quit writing about John Franco . . . I think his Nick Saban act has really damaged his regional reputation Franco won at Tyrone because he had great players and a lot of them. What happened at Tyrone was simply a case of blackmail. Give Franco the job he craved or he leaves for Altoona . . . This is all about John Franco and his pursuit of money.

In the end, Franco never applied for the position. For the Tyrone Golden Eagles who had played under him and who were disillusioned when they first learned of their fabled coach's departure, perhaps they too learned a lesson. That lesson was one in resiliency and faith in themselves, for as Franco posted two undesirable records at Altoona (albeit against formidable WPIAL completion), Tyrone proceeded to reach the second round of the District 6 playoffs two years in a row in his absence. During the 2014 season, both Tyrone under new head coach Jason Wilson and Altoona under Coach Franco posted winning results and playoff berths, with Wilson logging the Eagles' tenth district championship.

Despite the turmoil and politics, John Franco unquestionably was everything a brilliant coach needs to be—an organizer, a motivator, and a teacher. His coaching saga here may well be complete. With the resignation of successor coach Steve Guthoff after two seasons, the board publicized the head coach position opening per past practice. According to newspaper accounts,

Franco expressed interest in a return to Tyrone at that time, but in the final analysis he did not apply. Some conjectured that he would have considered the move had he received a call from the board or from the superintendent requesting that he apply, offering him some assurance that the votes were there to hire him. But this is purely conjecture—only John Franco can resolve the question with any authority.

Though it may have been the most publicized, Coach Franco's saga was certainly not the most politicized extracurricular crisis we dealt with through my years. During the 1993 board election year, when a famed leader of a conservative coalition was on the ropes (more on that figure in the next lessons) they conducted a desperate attack on our attempts to remove both the football coach and the band director from their positions. The rationales behind the removal of these employees were simple: the football coach had sketchy classroom control, and the band director had acted unprofessionally with a student. Simply put, we hired teachers first and coaches second—and we were not going to tolerate substandard instruction, even if the teacher had an undefeated season and was a terrific guy to boot. Likewise, a man who could not conduct his own professional behavior should not be conducting kids in a high school band. These principles sound patently traditional—they are the types of things a conservative voter wants to hear from school director candidates. Instead, the ultra-conservative coalition signed a letter to the editor of the *Herald* attacking our position on these two personnel issues. The coalition argued:

> Going back to the days of [Coach A], the coach—[he] came to us from another district where he was highly regarded as a coach and classroom teacher . . . but as soon as [Coach A] began referring students to Neil Smith for discipline he was made out to be a poor teacher and he was purged from the system at the recommendation of the principal. It is common knowledge that Mr. Smith is known as a wimp, incapable of dealing with the discipline within the school . . . Is it any wonder our football program is in the pits???

Ironically, just as these conservative school board candidates acted more in the manner of a teacher's union representative in protecting a questionable instructor, they promoted what amounted to a potentially illegal and certainly irresponsible agenda in protecting a band director who acted inappropriately with a student:

> Tyrone had a good playing band and a good competition band under [Abe]. Rumors were circulated by the Dynasty about [Abe's] morals. Were any charges filed by the Miller Dynasty for [Abe's]misconduct? No. [Abe]was threatened by an unsatisfactory rating by the administration. By using this leverage [Abe] was forced to resign and the Band went down the tube like the football program.

> How long will you people put up with this kind of treatment? You can do something about it. On November 2 vote for THE PEOPLE'S CHOICE.

The "People's Choice" quarter-page ad in the October 30, 1993 *Tyrone Daily Herald* illustrates how thoroughly politics blurred the lines between extracurricular pursuit and sound educational practice, so much so that sport and band could be deployed at will to attack entirely unrelated agenda items:

> **TO THE VOTERS IN THE TYRONE SCHOOL DISTRICT**
> It would be good to define the real issues in the November 2nd election of the school board candidates.

> For the last 18 months the Miller Dynasty have [sic] held a majority and have [sic] expressed their intentions! 20 months ago the People's Choice were[sic] in a majority and to economize and save the taxpayers a tax increase, there were cuts in administrative personnel. The Miller Board has now reinstated these administrators with handsome pay increases. As just one example—we now have a SUPERINTENDENT, an ASSISTANT SUPERINTENDENT, and an ASSISTANT to the SUPERINTENDENT . . . A 300% increase!!!

> After the April primary when friends of the Miller Dynasty were nominated, the majority on the board renewed the superintendent's contract 11 months

before its renewal date—and with a bonus of $6000. They also hired Joanne Lang, a friend of the superintendent, for $49,500—a $10,000 raise over a salary she had worked for Tyrone for 6 months earlier. And to make matters worse . . . the job was never advertised!!

Some people have postulated that . . . the band director, was unloaded as a smoke screen for the above two actions of the board, the 11-month early renewal of the superintendent's contract and $6000 raise and bringing back Joanne Lang with a $10,000 raise without advertising the job. These are things thoughtful voters should ponder.

Ad Paid for by—Tyrone School Director

Our political countermove was to answer the People's Choice accusations with accurate information in an ad that revealed their distortions and lies, for as Mark Twain pointed out, a lie can travel halfway around the world while the truth is putting on its shoes.

Whereas sometimes in this book I advocate lying low to allow public opinion to swell against hypocrisy and wrong-doing, or wait for fear to diminish with time and more information, here was an easy opportunity to separate myth from fact because the facts were matters of public record. We began by destroying the myth that the conservative coalition cut positions to save a tax increase. The fact was that there had been no tax increases for three years and that all positions were restored by the present board. The fuzzy 300% increase in salaries likewise had no basis in fact, for 1993-94 administrative salaries were actually less by $2,500 than the total amount paid in 1992-93 and less than the amount spent in 1991-92 by $39,500. Similarly, the 11-months-too-soon contract renewal charge, we pointed out, was in keeping with section 1073 of the Pennsylvania School Code, Manner of Election or Approval[5]. My contract expired in June of 1994 and could be renewed anytime from July 1, 1993 to January of 1994, but "at least 150 days prior to the expiration date of the term of office." As for the fantasy $6,000 bonus, I received no increase from 1991-92 to 1992-93, while a $4,069 raise was approved for 1993-94—a total three-year raise less than that received by the lowest paid

---

5 This refers to when a superintendent can be elected or reelected.

teacher in the school district over the previous two years. We pointed out also that I was paid less than the superintendents of both neighboring Bellwood-Antis and Spring Cove districts. Joanne Lang's raise was equally defensible, as she had been promoted from a principal/special education coordinator to an assistant superintendent / curriculum coordinator / director of special education—a multi-hat position that at some districts (depending on the size) still requires two or three people to fill. Lang had also moved from a 195 day to a 233 day contract, further justification for her raise. The band director, whose "unloading," according to the People's Choice Coalition, was all a "smoke screen" to deflect public attention away from our administration's shameless money grab, voluntarily resigned. This resignation was unanimously accepted by the board well before the election—accepted even by the board members running the ads for the People's Choice who questioned our motives in dismissing him. Perhaps they should have stood up at board vote and rejected his resignation if they believed so firmly in his innocence. Either way, their write-in campaign failed, with the incumbents winning by a decisive 2 to 1 margin and restoring the focus of our mission to educate kids.

Perhaps it is because our own childhoods are so intertwined with sport, play, imagination and music that we value teams, competition, and the arts so intensely in our schools. Inexorably, for good or ill, our own ambitions and egos become projected onto our children. For better or worse, sports and the arts can teach us how to work together—or how to tear each other apart. They can teach us the dignity and humanity that emerge from creative endeavor and by playing fair and clean—or the degradation that comes from fighting dirty.

Such lessons cannot be learned in classrooms, of course—another reason why the politically aware superintendent would do well to keep the ABC's in proportionate perspective to their weight in developing whole students.

Principles of Prevailing

- ✓ It is because our own childhoods are so intertwined with sport, play, imagination and music that we value teams, competition, and the arts so intensely in our schools.
- ✓ Many of the public will never be as enamored of academic successes and endeavors as they will be of extracurricular ones. Appreciate their enthusiasm nonetheless.

✓ Appropriate adequate funding for athletics, band, and chorus without sacrificing fiscal and academic integrity.
✓ Never allow booster groups to overwrite board policies or principles.
✓ Academic and athletic successes will feed off each other—but only if you hire high-quality staff to nurture those successes.

"Those who say religion has nothing to do with politics do not know what religion is."

—Gandhi

"When politics and religion are intermingled, a people is suffused with a sense of invulnerability, and in the gathering speed in their forward charge, they fail to see the cliff ahead of them."

—Frank Herbert, author of *Dune*

6 | Beware of Religion & Politics

A person whose values and will to power often occupied my waking hours and threatened the progressive health of our academic mission, has informed the conflicts discussed throughout this book. For many decades this man served as a vocational teacher in our school district, and then after his retirement, in his capacity as a school board member, as a leading force in many ultra-conservative coalitions. In this lesson, his fascinating and controversial power and politics will take center stage—if for no other reason than to illustrate how easy and dangerous it is for any individual's identity politics and regressive world view to gain root and attempt to grow in a small town's institutions and culture. This looming figure I am here pseudonymously naming Tom. Charles and Dave, (also being pseudonymously named) Tom's devoted followers and associates in religious absolutism and its effects on our school district's culture and school board's policy-making, are also major characters in this story.

Tom loved politics and was outspoken in his attempts to implement his political objectives. Among his close cadre of World War II veterans, he was a man of high ideals, unselfish with his time, and committed to helping his community. In his later years, however, according to first-hand accounts that I gleaned from the clients, colleagues, and family who knew him best, Tom became polemically more rigid, impatient, and argumentative as his career in education progressed. His tendency was like that of many politically-impassioned individuals of the Greatest Generation era: to reduce the gray complexities of politics to black-and-white absolutes, clinging resolutely to the entrenched biases and cultural mores of his formative years, either unable or unwilling to change with the tumultuous social upheaval of the sixties and beyond.

Tom's resistance to change was as evident in his classroom as it was in his political stance on issues like national defense and civil rights. He taught in Tyrone's in-house vocational program, primarily production agriculture. As such programs state-wide became more accepting state-wide of female students and ventured into curricula that focused more on agriscience, ecology, and advanced technology, Tom's program was restricted to boys—and the curriculum was restricted largely to pragmatic yet old-school concerns like equipment repair, traditional farming techniques, and crop rotation. Such restrictions in the face of widespread cultural change gradually precipitated the demise of his curriculum.

To thoroughly understand Tom's mind, consider a few observations from Fenwick W. English's *What They Didn't Tell You in Schools of Education about School Administration*. In the book, English contends that political and religious absolutists "pander to the need of the populace for certainty, not relative certainty, but *absolute certainty!*" In other words, one thing that the absolutist cannot tolerate is doubt—which, to the absolutist, makes an age of nuclear weaponry, climate change, and geopolitical flux immeasurably distressing. The political and religious absolutist in particular wants a promise of security in his ever-changing world—and that's where many ultra-conservatives and book-burners step in—with the promise of Certainty, with black-and-white Solutions, with clear lines of Good and Evil. Paradoxically, those who demand certainty may be the most egregious doubters of all, and they have what English calls "the greatest need for an antidote." For the absolutist, a Koran or a Bible is not true more or less; it is 100% true, and literally so, since figurative interpretations as required by parable, symbol, and allegory can lead to wild and crazy theological notions.

When applied to education, the need for certainty manifests itself in curriculum struggles over creationism and evolution—with scientific and scriptural apologists alike retreating to their corners for absolute proof of their positions, despite the fact that science falls as short as scripture in supplying definitive answers to life's greatest enigmas. The Uncertainty Dilemma of the absolutist also thrusts its way into the administration of our schools, for Black reminds the reader that absolutists are not content to "have just *The Catcher in the Rye*—they want the whole curriculum"—and that includes the curriculum shapers and policy makers.

Perhaps Tom fit the profile of the absolutist—of one who cannot tolerate religious or political ambiguity, of one who seems incredibly certain about everything yet is inwardly unsure of much, of one who promises a world free of doubt. Understanding Tom's psychological complexity and the degree to which he visibly cared about public schools as institutions that shape society, I approach his portrayal with sensitivity. I would be remiss, however, if I did not confess how difficult it was in writing and rewriting this lesson to maintain authorial objectivity about Tom. To many of his friends and relatives, whose extensive interviews with me revealed how much they loved and respected Tom, his political positions were disconcerting.

To illustrate Tom's thoroughness in ensuring that black-and-white religious and political principles (exclusively Christian ones) informed our school, consider the following transcript of a job interview he conducted on January of 1992. At this time, the board consisted of a 5-4 majority and was grilling prospective speech therapist Rosalind Tate with questions that were as patently illegal then as they are now. As early as 1988, a Tom-led minority faction of the school board claimed that it was their right as elected board members to interview teacher candidates in making "value judgments." This interview was perhaps typical of all those conducted by Tom's interview committee, in that no administrators were permitted to participate, nor were administrators permitted to attend, any meetings that the board conducted with faculty regarding curriculum development:

Tom: What is your opinion about the Bible in school?

Rosalind Tate: The reason the Bible is not allowed in the schools is because we cannot favor one religion over another. We are dealing with a secular system where children come from different backgrounds. You not only have Christians but you have Jews, Muslims, etc. That is why there are Christian academies and parochial schools. If someone is concerned about religion being a part of his child's education, then he has the option of sending his child to a religious affiliated school.

Tom: I see here you are very active in your church. Please explain.

Rosalind Tate: I'm involved in various aspects . . . Presently, I'm a member of the pastoral council and family life committee.

Tom: What's that about?

Aside from a single inquiry regarding her ability to handle a significant case load, the interview was devoid of any direct, speech therapy-related questions unearthing whether Mrs. Tate could teach her subject. It was with such ideological tunnel-vision that Tom's vocational program enrollment under his tenure had atrophied to single digits at its nadir, with most students serious about a solid program choosing not to enroll. While other teachers shared Tom's ideologies, they were much more covert in conveying and implementing them, as they understood as perhaps he did not the ethical and often legal ramifications of proceeding publically with their single-minded absolutism.

In a May 3, 1991 letter to the *Tyrone Daily Herald* editor, principal Neil Smith outlined Tom's shortcomings, among them that he only "*reluctantly* agreed to comply with title IX" in allowing female students into his vocational program and that his enrollment had dropped to a nadir of "2 students" after failing to attract any more than 11 at its height. Smith pointed out that the content of Tom's elective "cannot be verified, as the required course guide was never turned in to Mr. Westley." What is more, his course did not even meet the number of hours needed to qualify as a vocational program in the state. While some of his former students recall him as an effective disciplinarian, and honest gentleman, and an authoritative advisor on agricultural matters, the man clearly did as he wished when he wished, eschewing any paperwork that might define or demand his personal accountability, district and state documenting mandates be damned. On one occasion, he brooked school policy by taking his students on an unauthorized field trip to Huntingdon to meet a political figure, even allowing some of his students to drive their own cars with students, a clear liability blunder. On occasion, according to a former student, he would direct a class of students to begin work on a specific project—and then simply abandon them to do his politicking either on-campus or off-campus during class time. All of this noncompliance with administrative directives seemed ironic when, as a board member, Tom directed principal Neil Smith to hand over all of his teacher observations, an infringement of ethical behavior and an intrusion on professional relationships that Mr. Smith had established within his school.

Certainly, the agenda that Tom attempted to execute as a teacher he eventually tried to carry through as a school board member—and with a sense of mission rooted as much in the tenets of his politics as in his personal vendettas. He blazed through curricular, staffing, and financial decisions without conducting a single feasibility study. Not only did he support firing everyone from the athletic director and building principal to the assistant superintendent (whose post he refused to fill) and the superintendent (eight positions in all), he and his key supporter Charles considered firing the district's solicitor, seeking instead one who would not support me if the board should ever decide to take me to court. Eventually the board agreed to continue with solicitor Mike Dorezas on a temporary basis only. The elementary librarian had to go, too—most likely because she took the "liberal" stance in supporting challenged books. All of the cuts, of course, were surgically vindictive like this, intended to cut out people—not just positions. It is very likely that the attempt to cut Pete Dutrow's athletic director position, for instance, was bred from an altercation at a high school basketball game at which a high school teacher who was serving as time-keeper got into verbal and physical contact with Charles, who was later elected to the board. Charles demanded a written apology for his ejection from the event at the hands of Athletic Director Pete Dutrow, who escorted him out the door. Neither Mr. Dutrow nor the district apologized for the manner in which the situation was addressed. Similarly, the Tom group dismissed student-friendly programs like the Academic Spotlight at board meetings—no longer would the board room be a venue for celebrating the excellence of our students and staff. Such celebrations could be conducted elsewhere. With enough rope, the Tom coalition eventually hanged itself with anti-student and faculty procedures such as these.

I can trace back Tom's stance toward me to an incident that transpired shortly after I became superintendent. It was brought to my attention that Tom never turned in travel expenses. He would teach half a day, and then he was assigned to circulate to the residences of his students—as is still the practice of teachers with similar vocational assignments. Because Tom never turned in travel expenses, we had only a nebulous idea of what he was doing or where he was going. In short, Tom had no accountability in regard to how he was spending his time when he was not in his classroom as a teacher. To increase accountability, I required that he provide the district with expense vouchers that would help to document his time. Tom expressed clear aversion to this request, bristling at the prospect that the accountability measures would allow the District to "know my business."

Tom acquiesced to the request, but the final straw for him was near his retirement when we continued to see the enrollment in his department drop, perhaps because of the biased manner in which he discouraged female students from enrolling in his program—and perhaps because of his emphasis on politicking at the expense of teaching his subject. Based on these trends, I met with Tom and told him that he would be working only as a part-time teacher, working half days. This pronouncement forced his retirement, and we later hired an outstanding educator who within a year resurrected the program into one of the strongest agricultural-vocational programs in central Pennsylvania.

Had I appeased Tom and let him retire on his own terms, I might have done the expedient thing and avoided an ensuing decade of political retaliation from Tom's seat as a school board member with a fire in his belly. I could have allowed him to disguise his increasingly obsolescent program as a bona fide vocational training course for a few more years—or until enrollment eventually laid a goose egg. But one cannot condone expedience when the best interests of students are at stake.

So I acted, and sometimes in doing so, we have to pay for it later. Soon, Tom organized his bitterness toward me and the entire "Miller Dynasty," as his followers dubbed it. Tom's group had momentum, for he had been beating his drum since the 1980's, saying that the Tyrone Area School District Board was controlled solely by me (and previously by my father Norman)—for a combined span of at least fifty years. A retired Tyrone teacher at one point wrote a letter to Governor Shapp, who referred it to Harry Gerlach with the Department of Education. The teacher, William Artman, stated that I was not superintendent certified and that the board had not even considered other applicants. In essence, the claim was that I was rubber-stamped into the position because of my father's connection. He requested that the Department of Education investigate not only my accreditation but also the school's budget and all of the other "corruption" that was taking place in Tyrone. So Tom's group had context on which to build.

In a twisted gesture of making the personal political, Tom launched his decades-long grudge in the form of censorship attacks, of obstructionist tactics thwarting school consolidation, of tax reform measures and other bullet points prominent on the conservative national agenda. What was so patently obvious about this agenda, however, was not its political bent, which was to be expected, but the personal retribution with which it was administered. You have to grow a thick skin to respond to animosity when appropriate and to ignore it until the right moment. For instance, when my father was preparing to retire as superintendent, there was a mocking, unsigned letter circulated around town that actually backfired on those who published it, but in the tract we were satirically dubbed the "Poor Miller Family." Our family was in transition, of course, with my father's retiring. An excerpt follows, replete with both anti-communist innuendo and anti-Miller invective:

> All of us are asked to help those less fortunate than we and most of us give a helping hand when we can. This is another letter of appeal. This time it is for the Norman Miller Family.
>
> You see the Miller Family is going to have a transition period to face in the near future . . . and has had up to five of its family members in the employment of the Tyrone School System, two of them grossing over $35,000. To step down from this kind of income to Social Security or unemployment compensation would in fact be ONE BIG STEP. It is conceivable that Mother Catherine may not be able to go on her pilgrimages to "Mother Russia" and may even have to go second class and travel in the United States, a hardship for someone like her who can't even speak the native language of our people yet.
>
> Another unbearable thought would be where, other than Tyrone, could Billy Miller find such a lush salary with so few talents? A lot of good teachers

who had the experience of living on a lot less than Billy now gets could make a change because good teachers are always in demand but the unemployment list of poor administrators is long.

We could go on and on reciting the reasons why you should dig deep now and help the Miller Family, but we are sure you have some of your own reasons, so do what you think is right. Just write your checks to Norman Miller and mail to:

Poor Miller Family
5th Street
Tyrone, PA

My mother Catherine Miller was especially aggrieved by the attack. Still, the letter hit a nerve with a lot of people and typified the intensity of the sentiments that a few townspeople harbored toward my family.

But Tom's eventual command over the board majority did not happen instantaneously. In fact, in 1988, the vote was 7-2 to give me a five-year contract. Tom was outspoken with his initial political ally Julie about my contract, claiming in the *Altoona Mirror* that the district should not "perpetuate a dynasty." Within the year, however, Tom's sphere of influence had gained critical mass, enlisting voices like that of Charles, who wrote the following in the *Altoona Mirror*, an inflammatory editorial enumerating what he perceived to be fiscal shortcomings and missteps in the 1989 proposed budget, ignoring all the while Tyrone's featherweight school tax burden:

Tyrone's One-Man Board

Because of the $1.2 million increase over the last school term, the board will vote to increase the taxes of residents . . . William Miller said he felt uncomfortable with only a possible $782 balance in the general fund.

Why should he be uncomfortable about anything? Two weeks ago he and he alone presented an almost $8 million budget to the school board. Whatever happened to the so-called "finance committee" that we created two years ago?

I'm sure the majority of taxpayers in this area would feel more comfortable if our school board applied some common sense and cut expenses by eliminating a couple administrative positions . . . and then cut back on the rest of the administrative salaries by 5 percent.

I'm surprised someone hasn't suggested dissolving the school board—but then that would expose the "one-man system," wouldn't it . . . It's enough to give people who live within a budget and who really believe in positive education a bad case of WORMS.

By 1991, in no small part due to the inherent political and cultural conservatism of our town, Tom had marshaled enough political invective and mass to ensure my ouster. He had convinced a majority on the board that the district had "been dominated by a monolithic bureaucracy" and that the new board "reflects a new ideology and Miller doesn't fit that ideology." Tom demanded a meeting with teachers to amplify the urgency of his agenda. Almost immediately, he demanded (flouting the board-approved school calendar) that the students be let out early despite the bus problems and the child-care entanglements that his grand gesture would create for families. Turning a shoulder to students' needs, Tom was eager to rouse a broad audience and create maximum community buzz to explain why the administration must be cut and how teachers could profit outside the oppression of a totalitarian regime. Copies of national school board journals were to be available to all school directors so that they knew how to be more than suited marionettes with rubber stamps. All of this transpired in the context of a Sputnik-impassioned speech about the declining international competitiveness of American students, after which board member and parent Larrie Derman, fully aware of the propaganda-machinery that Tom once operated in the classroom, remarked, "I don't want you to inflict your trash on me . . . I don't want to hear a history lesson."

On Christmas Eve of 1991, the headline of the *Tyrone Daily Herald* read, "'New' School Board Votes To Request Miller's Resignation." Board member Harry Sickler had to remind the board that a superintendent could not be removed without cause. Still, the vote had been tied 4-4; the man who broke it was Dave.

While he was certainly a man of his own mind—a true gentleman whom I fully respect and admire to this day—Dave was susceptible to Tom's agenda if not to his contentious brand of politics. I also believe that he knew in the end that the manner in which Tom tried to dismiss me was patently wrong and not encouraged by the most honorable motives—for Dave too had suffered publically and privately in his attempts to do what he earnestly thought was in the best interests of students.

Dave initially gained public exposure at the fore of attempts to ban literature in senior high classrooms. Dave's ally Charles and Reverend Jack had initiated their own campaigns against the English curriculum, assailing classics by Steinbeck, Heller, Vonnegut, and many others by making unscheduled visits to classrooms and writing letters to the governor's office to pressure teachers to purge their classrooms of "trash" like *Of Mice and Men* and *Catch-22*.

Charles visited local businesses and manufacturing facilities as well with political machinations. At one point, 130 people attended a board meeting, most of them supporting the removal of Joyce Carol Oates' classic short story "Where Are You Going, Where Have You Been?" In their defense, many of these attendees had been enflamed by packets of isolated literary excerpts photocopied and circulated to employees at the Chicago Rivet Company. They simply had not read the original works. Most contained mild profanity expected in modern literature from Steinbeck and Heller. Some of the circulated excerpts, however, were brazenly pornographic in their depictions of sex. It did not help the cause of the Dave coalition that these graphic depictions were from titles not taught in our schools. Instead of passages from Elie Weisel's classic autobiographical holocaust account *Night*, a work free of any semblance of profanity and sexual content, one censorship advocate distributed racy tidbits from a lurid novel of the same title, never checking to see which novel the district actually taught.

A library review committee was established to review such concerns, but Dave was disenchanted with the committee's majority opinion:

> When characters in fiction use profanity, this does not mean that the author or the teacher advocates the use of such language. By eleventh grade, it seems reasonable to assume that students can distinguish when a particular type of language is appropriate and when it is not.

Dave called the work of the committee "ineffective and invalid" because those that were involved were either proponents of the books in question or else school administrators. He called it a "no-win situation" in which the school appeared to be trying to resolve the situation "on the surface" and had already decided to keep Oates' work in the curriculum. He gave an impassioned four-minute speech during the school board meeting and at the end received a standing ovation.

"You're breeding a tax revolt!" shouted a resident named Joe who had been placed on the agenda to speak on taxes. He told the board that they must take action on books in the school system because taxpayers had demanded it.

When Board President James Kimmel reminded the resident that he must stick to the topic of taxes, Joe rebutted to cheers and whistles, "Now you're trying to censor me!"

I respected Dave because I felt that his faith was sincere. He was employed with an auditing firm, and he eventually became a partner. During a deposition regarding the Devon financial crisis, Dave furnished memoranda received from his partners in early 1992 raising questions regarding his openness and the nature of his controversial views as a school board member. The memos detailed how those views had affected his firm, with political protestors at one point picketing about school affairs at the front door of his establishment. Ultimately, Dave stated that he was willing to sacrifice his $100,000 per year job with his firm in a values-driven commitment of time and effort to his position on the Tyrone Area School Board. Such a sacrifice cannot help but command respect.

It was at the first board meeting after Dave was elected an officer that the request for my resignation was made. Shortly after the board meeting, I asked for a meeting with Dave in my office because I felt it was very important for the school programs, the students, and the future of the community that we meet. I had followed this past practice with such officers. We discussed President Bush's number-one goal about starting school ready to learn, about intervention projects, and about the long-range plan of our elementary school facility, the feasibility study, the negotiations committee, and that he was hoping to collapse the assistant superintendent position, saving well over $100,000. During this meeting, he told me how difficult it was for him to vote for my resignation that night, particularly when my family was sitting there in the front row. However, after that meeting, it was determined, apparently by other board members in his group that he would no longer meet with me individually and that he would only agree to meet if he and other board members were present. I understood, and I appreciated his sensitivity and humanness in acknowledging my family's plight.

Dave's own plight piqued as a result of a lawsuit brought against him by the former pastor of his fledgling church. Dave and his wife were trustees of the church that had removed Reverend Donald Campbell. Campbell originally was intensely popular with some in his congregation. Former Tyrone councilwoman Dorothy Thomas said Campbell was the type of man who could "call down miracles." Thomas claimed that she once took her son on a camping trip on which they had no bread. Reverend Campbell told the kids to "pray for bread"—and in New Testament "loaves and fish" fashion, along came a bread truck. Thomas, like many, grew disenchanted after Campbell eventually took out loans to renovate the property, albeit with his own sweat equity, and later claimed title to the building which had once been a target of spray-painted graffiti like "Satan Rules." Campbell also claimed the congregation owed him more than $10,000 for unreimbursed repairs. He contacted Philadelphia attorney Angel Franqui to sue both Dave and his wife as trustees to recover his renovation funds. In a letter to Campbell, Franqui wrote:

> In speaking to several witnesses, I learned that [Dave] is somewhat of a local celebrity in Tyrone. Recent newspaper articles seem to indicate that he has also taken over the Tyrone school board and is attempting to oust its longstanding, loyal administration, eliminate its athletic programs, and segregate girls and boys. Your differences with him are not an isolated case.

The suit against Dave was eventually dropped amid allegations that Franqui was an acquaintance of my family. Dave charged in the *Altoona Mirror* that "there is no doubt in my mind [that the suit] was politically motivated." This, of course, was not accurate. Franqui did call me at one point to state that Campbell had contacted him to file the suit—and he said that he thought that the suit might help me. I never contacted Franqui nor requested any action or support from him. Ultimately, Franqui explained to *Altoona Mirror* reporter Chiffon Wells that Campbell dropped the suit because he "didn't want to go through with it, possibly because of the gossip."

Eventually, the Tom coalition was sunk by the legal and religious quagmire surrounding the church combined with the backlash over censorship attacks and the wholesale dismantling of two administrative and six teaching staff posts. Many residents were embarrassed that their town was being lampooned in local news accounts in cartoonish fashion. One of those lampoons from

The Tyrone Daily Herald dated May 21, 1992 was directed at the group under the title of "School Board Poetry," replete with puns on Tom's surname and gibes about his brand of Christian salvation:

> "School Haze"
> The Major Five are all upset,
> They've been misunderstood.
> They only want to starve our schools . . .
> They want to save them good.
> And so they always act as one,
> In secret if they can—
> Their leader's name is [Tom] Scrooge,
> A most determined man.
> It's strange how those who would do good
> Can end up doing wrong.
> "School Haze, School Haze"
> Is this group's favorite song.

A previous lampoon appeared in the *Altoona Mirror* as a political cartoon. Perhaps it was this cartoon that presaged Tom's fate, so scathing it was in encapsulating the politics of the moment and sparking community embarrassment. It featured an unsmiling, puritanical figure with a buckled pilgrim's hat holding a traditional *First Grade Reader*. The tagline above read: "Meanwhile, at the Tyrone League of Decency . . ." Beneath the Puritan the caption read, "Let my kids read this? No way. Here are this Dick and Jane—unmarried, no less—cavorting without shame! And who's this Spot? Why isn't he wearing any clothes? What kind of sick ménage-a-trois is this?"

After all was said and done, after all in the Tom group were no longer in power on the board, Dave came of his own volition to my office, where he apologized to me. I shook his hand.

He gave me a hug. He had experienced a very difficult time dealing with the political and emotional trauma of his unofficial membership in the Tom coalition. While I saw him as a true believer, driven foremost by his religious convictions, it also seemed as if he and many like him had become in the process a tool of Tom's regressive politics and ill-will.

The same can be said of other Tom disciples, including Charles and Julie. Julie promised an era of openness and transparency. Charles was a Tom disciple for sure—in politics, athletics, and religion. Most folks remember Charles for his religious fervor and the extremist slant of his curricular decision-making. An editorial in the April 28, 1992 *Tyrone Daily Herald* entitled "Clowns" satirized Charles's extremism:

> Once again Tyrone is feeling the brunt of ridicule. Now not only is it known throughout the state as a town of clowns which regularly shreds Borough Managers, it has now attained the dubious distinction of being a town which wants to drag its school system back into the age of chastity belts, book burnings, and puritanism . . .
>
> Witness the actions of the Majority Mafia on the Tyrone Area School Board. What has been state-mandated for years is suddenly adjudged a "sin." Guidance counselors are being cut and administrators being dumped in a vendetta against a superintendent who is being stalked with all the subtlety of an Elmer Fudd trying to get Bugs Bunny.
>
> The Majority Mafia has not once mentioned the students to whom they owe their first responsibility. All their machinations only thinly disguise their real purpose—a contract out on Dr. William Miller.

Not long after the editorial appeared, a political cartoon appeared in the local paper depicting an anonymous school board member.

"I want to bury the hatchet!" the board member says to the figure seated beside him at a board meeting.

The figure beside him has no chance to accept the truce, however, for all the reader sees are the soles of his shoes. The rest of his body is slumped behind the table, stone dead.

"Oops!" chortles the board member, who I believe was Dave but could have as easily been Charles in mind and spirit, "Sorry, Dr. Miller."

As much fun as the press was having over Dave's and Charles's one-minded world-view, there was scant laughter about it in the classrooms, offices, and hallways of our school district. As a matter of fact, laughter in the boardroom, as the April 19, 1992 *Altoona Mirror* reported, was grounds for throwing out an audience member. After chastising board members for outlawing recording devices and laughter, the editor wrote:

> Imagine! Boys and girls actually playing games together and learning about hygiene and bodily functions together! It's positively shameless . . . Does [Charles] actually believe that playing kickball and tag or running races puts children in jeopardy of unwanted pregnancy? . . . He would rather not have sex education in school at all. That's right: He would rather kids learn about sex and birth control in a more discreet fashion, like in the back seat of a car.

Chiffon Wells reported in a May 17, 1992 *Altoona Mirror* article that Charles believed "he not only answers to the public, but his actions as a school member will affect his immortal soul. On May 12, he told a crowd of more than 400 people that he has to answer to God for his decisions . . . describing mixed physical education and health classes as 'a sin' and 'immoral.'" In a *Herald* editorial, Dr. Kathryn Lewis previously questioned Charles's logic of requiring that girls have a designated female gym and sexual education teacher after Charles proposed terminating a female guidance counselor position. If girls needed female-led instruction in the classroom and the gymnasium, should they not also need female-led counseling sessions to discuss issues such as pregnancy, menstruation, or sexual abuse? Such misguided moral action eventually inspired Dr. Lewis' husband, the Reverend Samuel T. Lewis, to set up a lawn chair directly behind Charles's political inspiration, Tom—at a board meeting—just to let him know what he thought about his politics and his lies. In a subsequent personal letter to Tom, Reverend Lewis concluded that the school board member's

> . . . present actions are motivated by personal revenge pure and simple . . . an embarrassment to the whole community.
>
> The Bible says—"Revenge is mine, I will repay, saith the Lord."
>
> The Lord has ways of dealing with people who use His Name in behalf of their own ends.

Even in areas that Charles valued dearly—like athletics—he acted with a zealotry that made sports editors and athletic directors across central Pennsylvania wince. A baseball aficionado, Charles saw inherent value in sport, especially as a means to keep young folks busy and "off the streets." At a local YMCA basketball game, one could not mistake the spirited intersection of Charles's religious and athletic fervor as he broke into cheerleader mode, standing before the crowd and shouting zealously, "Gimme a Y! Gimme an M! Gimme a C! Gimme an A! What's that C stand for? Christian! Christian! Christian!"

Given this, *Altoona Mirror* sports editor Neil Rudel struggled to understand how such a sports enthusiast could consider terminating an athletic director position occupied by one of Tyrone's most vaunted coaches and educators, Pete Dutrow. No more than a month after Dutrow was recognized as Athletic Director of the Year in the Northwest Pennsylvania region comprising Districts 5, 6, 9, and 10, Charles recommended axing his job. Rudel asked rhetorically what possible justification there could be, and then he offered a two-word answer: the board's "sheer stupidity." Rudel pointed out that the vote to cut Dutrow's post was not even legal according to the Department of Education, which mandates that a majority of the board—not a majority of those present—was necessary. Absent an athletic director, Charles proposed that the coaches assume the duties of the director—woefully ignorant of the endless hours involved in schedule arrangements, weather tracking, communications, transportation, facilities preparation, event staffing, equipment procurement, media responsibility, record keeping, and eligibility documentation. Rudel pointed out that every other school in Blair County allotted at least a portion of the workday for an athletic director to execute his duties.

Charles's slash-and-burn fervor touched every corner of the curriculum, and his top-down approach was at diametric odds with the 1989 platform on which he ran—which was to see that teachers enjoyed working and that taxpayer money was spent properly. During the election, he felt that teachers were not involved enough in setting curriculum even though they were qualified in this area. Despite Charles's teacher-empowering rhetoric, it was over the vocal objections of the math department that he pushed foreign math programs like Kumon and Amon (which stressed abstract rote learning) over Saxon's math program, which emphasized real-world experience and concrete, varied materials. That the foreign programs were nearly four times as expensive as Saxon did not deter him. Concurrently, he made intimidating, unscheduled visits to English classrooms with Reverend Jack, threatening teachers that he would have to explore "other tactics" to remove pornographic authors like Vonnegut, Oates, and Steinbeck from the curriculum if teachers did not remove them expeditiously. Charles claimed at least twenty books in the department were pornographic, though at a 1999 deposition regarding the Devon fraud case he could name only one.

Charles was a political thorn years after his tenure on the board ended, especially in his Devon deposition with Attorney Jeff McFadden. Attorney Mike Betts prepared Charles's testimony, a retrospective of Charles's full time on the board and his lingering distrust and disdain for my style of leadership—if not for me personally. In the deposition, Charles indicated that he was encouraged to run for the board because the incumbent school directors blindly accepted the word of administrators concerning the work ethic of teachers. He supported a back-to-basics curriculum and claimed that Tyrone graduated students who could neither read nor write. The deposition posited that a dangerous aspect of Charles's political philosophy was that it might resonate with jurors. Jurors might identify with a school director who stands up to administrators, opposes pornography, wants to know where the money is being spent, and demands that kids be taught the basics.

Charles did not support the construction projects and claimed that I disdained oversight of any sort, preferring instead a puppet school board. He insinuated that I lied to him about the construction costs when I could not instantaneously quote him the difference in state reimbursement resulting from remodeling our schools versus new construction. He strenuously disagreed with my position that a superintendent was vested with the authority to make investments on behalf of his district, recalling that the transfer of money to Devon occurred in February of 1991 without my telling the board beforehand, instead advising the board after the fact. He testified that he had consulted an attorney who told him that I had broken the law, but Charles refused to identify the attorney, claiming that his identity was not important. Despite all of the insinuation and mischaracterization, of critical importance to the district's exoneration was Charles's admission through his deposition that when he left the board he did not believe that Tyrone's investments with Devon were at risk, that Black had engaged in unethical trading, or that I was aware of any unethical trading through Devon.

Nonetheless, the upshot of his testimony was that I initiated the investment with Devon based upon the representation that Devon was not charging any administrative fees. Fees were charged but then refunded to the district, and Charles expected that these refunds were evidence of my unqualified support of Black and of my recklessness to put the district in harm's way for a friend. The deposition summary by Mike Betts predicted that Charles's testimony would be discounted because of his dim understanding of the legal issues encompassing the investments and his "void of effort" to understand Mid-State Bank's fiduciary role and obligation. For instance, Charles thought that all public school investments were required to be FDIC-insured and that a superintendent and business administrator could only make temporary investments in T-bills or savings accounts. Charles said that I should have looked to an outside party to oversee district investments. He claimed that our solicitor Michael Dorezas approved the investments, which was not true; Dorezas only reviewed them.

Characteristic of his zealous approach to athletics and religion, in the end it was Charles's zeal to incriminate me that discredited his testimony. Charles courted *Wall Street Journal* reporter Michael Moss who was in and out of my office for over a week or two, as was news-hawk Mike Bucsko from the *Pittsburgh Post-Gazette*. Charles attempted to persuade these papers to attack me as best they could. Not only did these fellows pester me for weeks, but they also demanded follow-up interviews and written responses to on-going questions. *NBC Nightly News* even made the rounds through Tyrone on June 30, 1998 to plan a story on the whole affair. As Bucsko reported:

> Steve Beals, a former Tyrone mayor, summed up the feelings of many . . . "We're pissed."

> Surprisingly, the anger [over the Black case] is not aimed as much at Black as it is at Miller, 55, the school superintendent for 26 years. Some residents refer to Miller's tenure as the "Miller Dynasty" because his father, Norman, was superintendent for 32 years . . . There have been battles over neighborhood school closings, book bannings, and the districts investments with Black.

> "This time, the animosity has become a "personal vendetta", Miller said. "There's a deep-seated resentment bordering on hatred."

Charles undoubtedly relished the media rush and had even contacted Mid-State Attorney McFadden's office, "crazily claiming that Dr. Miller was running scared" by trying to schedule his deposition, which Tanya Sharer, my secretary, had scheduled at the request of the attorneys involved. He made spirited contacts with the governor, with the secretary of education, with anybody who would listen. "This was the most fertile testimony to establish [Charles]'s bias," reported Betts' deposition of Charles, "that he can be made to come across as a nut if he reveals his attempts to 'get' Dr. Miller."

Understandably, a few years after the Devon case, Charles's relationship with me was far from cordial, but despite the decades of political discord, a few years before his death Charles and I had gotten to the point where we could cross paths occasionally in town and exchange pleasantries. I have said many times that there is not enough room in my closet for grudges, and I certainly harbored none towards Charles. Like so many well-meaning board members, perhaps he had fallen under the influence of Tom's charisma. That Charles left this earth on speaking terms with a man he once called a liar and a criminal says much about the regenerative power of forgiveness—even in the seemingly soul-less world of school district politics.

In a narrow sense, politics is all about power. Power, most agree, can be defined as the ability to influence others, for better or worse. Therefore, when most folks contemplate the mechanics of political power, they immediately think Machiavelli—shrewd deception, ruthless retaliation, power hoarding, without necessarily exploring the ways that abuses of power rob us of spiritual growth. Power hoarding kills the spirit rather than liberates it. Power must be shared to advance the cause of good in the world, so leading while sharing power is essentially an act of giving. As Lee Bolman argues in *Leading with Soul*, "If leaders clutch power tightly, they reactivate old patterns of antagonism . . . Conflict is often suppressed, [but] eventually it emerges in coercive or explosive forms." This is what happened in the explosive years of the haughty, power-hoarding school board directed and controlled by Tom. Dedicated individuals like Julie were swept up in the charisma and religious message of the board. With the passage of time, Julie and I have become friends and always speak with each other at social gatherings. A brief hug shared at such occasions reinforces for me how easily politics and religion can both unify and divide.

It's a twist on a simple Christian paradox: "Blessed are the meek, for they shall inherit the earth." The way to expand one's power is to give it away—judiciously, of course. Doing so requires incredible faith—in oneself, in colleagues, in the mission, and in God. Doing so will not make one powerless—for if power corrupts, powerlessness is even more corrosive. Giving away power is an act of love, as our work is really an act of love.

Principles of Prevailing

- ✓ When applied to education, the religious or political absolutist's need for certainty usually manifests itself in curriculum struggles over scientific theories and books.
- ✓ The absolutist is often not content to legislate a single theory or to alter just one book; he often wants to nix the whole curriculum—as well as the curriculum shapers and policy makers.

✓ Personal vendettas often drive the absolutist more passionately than does any particular dogma. These vendettas will get intensely personal. Prepare yourself—and your family—for them.

✓ Power hoarding kills the spirit rather than liberates it; power must be shared to advance the cause of good in the world, for leading is essentially an act of giving.

✓ If power corrupts, powerlessness is even more corrosive. Take charge.

✓ Be patient—absolutists will eventually extricate themselves.

✓ When that happens, try to make amends.

"If all printers were determined not to print anything till they were sure it would offend nobody, there would be very little printed."

—Benjamin Franklin

7 | Value Free Expression

Whether thwarting a censorship attack, structuring a parent advisory committee, delving to the bottom of a personnel matter, or listening to a student's blunt assessment of our schools, I have always attempted to elicit free expression. To do anything less is ethically, administratively, and politically dangerous—even if the words we hear are hard to take in.

The book banning saga was the earliest test of my will to foster free expression. The politically expedient course of action would have been to squelch the controversial materials quietly and recommend that teachers be more judicious in their future choice of materials. However, as the business of education is really the business of values, I could not choose expedience over principle. For all the angst they produced, the book banning attempts were educational experiences—and of the best variety, too, the kind that could never be replicated in a classroom. They were a civics lesson on the separation of church and state, a religious studies lesson on both New and Old Testament principles, and a literature lesson on authorial intent and contextual meaning, all wrapped into one—not just for students but for the entire community and for the school board.

Board member Carol Anderson summarized the civics lesson that emerged for her during the censorship crisis by declaring, "I think that my faith is just as strong as theirs, but I don't think it's right to parade it while I'm functioning as a government leader. My responsibility then is to weigh and represent all the interests of the people, not to crusade for moral change." Pastor Craig Faust of The Church of the Good Shepherd advocated a similar lesson. As Faust responded to a reporter, "As a Christian and minister, I would love to force everyone to see things my way, but the beauty of Christianity is freedom of choice. I think that is the cornerstone of our government. You have to be careful not to cross the line, not to legislate morality." For resident Faith Brown, a letter to the editor expressed a religious studies lesson that the book banning campaign underscored. Brown quoted passages from a book that depicted graphic accounts of erotic sex, cannibalism, adultery, and infanticide before revealing that the book she was quoting was the Bible. "What I have done," Brown wrote, "is no different than what Dave has done before the school board. By quoting a book out of context, I have misled readers to believe that the book is evil." For some students, the saga was a lesson in persuasive techniques, as many of their voices were instrumental in swaying the tide of public opinion. Consider these January 15, 1990 editorial remarks from Tyrone High literature student Greg Bock, who used rhetorical and critical thinking skills that he later applied in his career as a newspaper reporter:

> If students cannot experience books that contain obscenities or questionable language, then they would not be able to read Geoffrey Chaucer's *The Canterbury Tales*, John Steinbeck's *The Grapes of Wrath*, Aldous Huxley *Brave New World*, Richard Wright's *Native Son* . . . Even Shakespeare's sonnets could be considered inappropriate. Should students never experience great works of literature because isolated parts of them contain uncouth language or references to sexual situations?

In a separate letter of April 17, 1992, after the book banning in English classes movement morphed into the gender-separation movement in gym classes, Greg added:

[Charles], you are as bad as the pornographer. Both of you degrade the body and sexuality until it is dirty, filthy, and smutty. Adam and Eve lived naked without shame in the Garden of Eden. Only after they ate the forbidden fruit did they find themselves in shame. Those students who play a game of co-ed volleyball at the high school during gym class are just playing volleyball. Maybe Freud would find something psychosexual about this scenario, but I don't.

It was students like Greg whom I fought so hard to defend during the crisis, especially as inimical letters like the one below were written to Governor Robert Casey:

My Dear Sir,

I am enclosing just a part of the filth that is being permitted to be used in the classrooms of the Public Schools in Tyrone, Penna.

I want you to know that with every ounce of my energy, I oppose the use of such filth in the School systems of Pennsylvania. I want to serve notice to you and to all those who serve me in Harrisburg that I oppose the use of one cent of my tax monies for the purchase of such filth nor for the salaries of those who would even consider teaching such filth.

If memory serves me correctly, is not immorality one cause still in the School Code for dismissal of a professional employee of a Public School District?

I anxiously await your reply!

Sincerely,
Pastor [Jack]
[Redacted] Church

The Governor did reply to Pastor Jack, with a clear reminder from Senior Program Advisor John Meehan in February of 1990 that the state does not endorse a set literature curriculum and that reading material is a matter of local—not state—control. Jack had been so relentless in his attacks on both literature and teaching staff that on March 2, 1990, PSEA legal representative Randall Rodkey took the initiative to draft the minister this cautionary response:

> The issue of whether or not you have ever had a valid cause for complaint as to classroom materials is now no longer the issue. This has been lost sight of in your generalized, slanderous attack against the entire teaching staff and, in fact, the administrative staff of the School District . . .
>
> Your communications in this regard constitute actionable libel against each and every member of the professional staff . . . you are firmly advised that if you persist in this type of conduct, you will be exposing yourself to legal action for libel or slander of those involved.

Jack sheepishly backed away from his offensive after Rodkey had fired this litigious shot across his bow. However, two weeks later the minister drafted a letter to Board President James P. Kimmel indicating that his discontent was not with teachers, whom he previously had accused of everything from corruption of minors to homosexuality, but with the school board and with me. In that letter, Jack implied that I controlled both the board and the teachers in marionette fashion, even forcing teachers, in his version of reality, to attend board meetings to show their support of book selection policy:

> I never planned to name any teachers . . . When I learned from the Legal Community of Pennsylvania that one's personal life after school hours . . . cannot be used to discredit that individual . . . I immediately communicated with you. Believe me, that is the truth . . . The entire [school board meeting] was just a demonstration of the total control one man has over the majority of the School Board as well as over the over-qualified, super-competent teachers. What a tragedy!

Still, the defense of free expression was such a vital issue to the community that at one point during the crisis, Larry Stump, the head of the English department, spoke at a public meeting that had to be moved to the high school cafeteria because over

400 townspeople showed up—an amount equal to almost one out of every ten residents in the borough of Tyrone. Stump and Jack parried well for their respective supporters, with Jack defending the sanctity and the voice of family:

> I was born and raised in Tyrone. And I want to tell you tonight with God being my judge that the moral standards I have tonight were not taught to me in theological seminary but they were taught to me in the halls of Tyrone school system . . . I believe I know the ingredients of a quality education. And that's what I want for my teenagers and especially my grandson. The primary place God gives us is the family structure.

Each time Jack quoted scripture to defend his position, Stump quoted Scripture to defend his position, urging parents to "train up their children in the way that they should go." Stump reasoned that kids' solid home lives would shape their values, which could not be "undermined by a piece of literature intended to acquaint their children with a real life situation." Prior to this meeting I hired a personal lawyer, for Jack and his followers were attacking staff for dismissal on moral deficiency grounds, threatening to release a list of those he deemed morally deficient. Through the grapevine, I had heard that my name was at the top of Jack's list. At the meeting, perhaps noting my attorney, Jack changed his mind, for he named none of the parties on his "list."

A core group of Jack adherents fasted for a period of time prior to their election, asking God to place people in control of the board that were like-minded individuals. They prayed for victory, and they won on a platform of setting public schools free from controversial literature—a call to reform taxes, return to basics, and instill morality. Perhaps they felt that God had swayed their election—that the outcome was a direct result of their fasting and prayer, and that book banning was a mandate from God.

During their board tenure, they micromanaged every facet of district operations from personnel interviews to gender-based segregation in health classes. But with patience and perseverance on our part, some of our administrators prevailed. Neil Smith, our high school principal, entertained a lucrative job offer from a much wealthier district, but he chose to stay as a matter of principle and loyalty to the community in order to fight the Tom and Jack coalition and to help restore education in Tyrone to reasonable minds. Others like Joanne Lang actually moved ahead of the game from principal at Elizabethtown Elementary School and special education director at Tyrone to become principal at nearby Juniata Valley, knowing that she was on the Tom hit list. Likewise, Marion Homer, assistant high school principal, saw the handwriting on the wall and took a position elsewhere. As a public critic of Tom and company and because of her sexual orientation, Homer knew she would become a target. I admired Marion for her courage throughout this episode, in a time that was much more hostile than the present toward non-traditional lifestyles. Marion Homer had a great sense of humor, so I imagine that her cry for free expression might have sounded a lot like the one uttered by social satirist author Kurt Vonnegut when he wrote, "All these people talk so eloquently about getting back to good old-fashioned values. Well, as an old poop . . ., I say let's get back to the good old-fashioned First Amendment of the good old-fashioned Constitution of the United States—and to hell with the censors! Give me knowledge or give me death!" The high school librarian followed Homer's path and resigned, sensing that the library would be ground zero for the new board. Even award-winning band director Gerry Roberts announced at a public concert that he would retire because of the new board's priorities—particularly its bigotry.

So this crusade pitting the values of conservative Christian faith versus the national ethos of free expression was not without its victims. It was my personal consolation that none of those victims were students. Despite the brouhaha, most of the controversial works in our English department had never been required reading anyhow. They appeared on book lists that our teachers had recommended for personal enrichment. We subsequently made those lists available only upon student or parental request, though we continued to urge teachers to teach primary, unadulterated texts even as we also required them to clearly list in their syllabi possible parental objections to works with vulgarity or controversial content, along with suitable alternatives lest any assigned readings offend. These were common sense solutions. They demanded neither the lights of the media circus nor the fires of the witch hunt to enact.

However, as with so many areas of political engagement, one does not survive strictly by common sense. To ward off toxic forces in a district, sometimes sensible and active retaliation is in order, using the media to fight fire with fire. The Tyrone community fueled such engagement. Some of that retaliation came in the form of organized public meetings at local churches. Over 400 citizens packed the sanctuary of the Church of the Good Shepherd in May of 1992. A *Tyrone Daily Herald* account captured the duplicity of the Tom alliance that had promised increased openness but had instead banned the use of recording devices at school board meetings and ordered teachers "not to talk with students about the actions of the school board." As teacher Mark Nale joked at the media event, "This from the same [Julie] who said after the election that the era of fear and intimidation has come to an end." The Good Shepherd audience erupted into laughter.

But the scoffing did not deter Charles for long, for in May of 1993 he resurrected the book dispute by cutting the stipend of literary magazine advisor Steve Everhart, who had refused to move classics like *Brave New World* from his 11th grade in-class library after Charles had assailed this and several other works on Everhart's optional reading list three years prior. High school principal Neil Smith said that cutting the magazine was a personal vendetta, "an attempt to punish Everhart." Despite such setbacks and temporary regressions, the public meetings were enormously powerful. *Brave New World* still sits on the book-shelves in Tyrone High classrooms alongside other protested classics like *Of Mice and Men, Catch-22*, and *Fahrenheit 451.* Everhart, decades later the English Department chair, cannot recall the last time a complaint about these books has been filed, and the student literary magazine is more vibrant than ever.

The community ground gradually swelled against the degra-dation of education generated by Tom's coalition, which allowed me and other administrators in the district to position ourselves away from the fray as we watched and supported the citizens' counter rebellion. Groups like Lee and Rosemary Stover's Network of Concerned Citizens sprouted up in response. The mechanics of political backfire were similar when another grassroots group called Families for Quality Education engaged the community and staff in shedding light on Charles's inept micromanagement by taking out radio ads that highlighted his leadership debacles. With the involvement and commitment of Tyrone alumnus Tom Hoyne, a long-time supporter of the public school system, the political scales began to tip the other way with his connection to Rod Wolfe, whom Janette Kelly also helped to enlist in the cause. Rod Wolfe, owner of the WRTA radio station and Chair of the Republican Party in Blair County, joined us in the effort as we prepared for the primary election against the Charles group in 1993. Simultaneously, Doc Heeley, Chair of the Democratic Party, joined in the endeavor. So we had two keen minds from opposing political parties and Tom Hoyne, all supporting our cause. An organizer of literally thousands of campaigns, Wolfe endorsed our effort to marshal mass telephone calls to all registered voters to explain our positions and supportive candidates. The ad scripts along with the phone calls touched a nerve with enough folks to turn the tide against the Charles group, who had spearheaded attempts to put no fewer than eight positions on the chopping block, potentially crippling the district if he had his way—all in the name of fiscal responsibility and morality. The following spots capture well the flavor of Wolfe's campaign:

Spot #1:
Each time it ends up costing more money to bail ourselves out of the mess. Remember the high school boiler that was thirty years old? [Charles] ignored the professional's advice and opted for repairing the boiler on a piece-meal basis. The result? Same old boiler, but the piece-meal repair has almost doubled our heating costs to $60,000. Thanks, [Charles]. It's time for a change.

Spot #2:
Penny wise and pound foolish—that's [Charles's]way of saving money. Remember the auto-shop teacher fiasco? [Charles] didn't want to pay the recommended salary for a full-time auto-shop teacher. The result? Tyrone students had to suffer through four months without a full-time teacher? Were the kids the losers? You bet. Our students deserve better than a [Charles]calling the shots. You decide. It's your school system, not [Charles].

Spot #3:
Last year [Charles] said the best way to save money was to fire and reassign personnel in the Tyrone school system. [Charles] never consulted anyone to see what would happen. And he didn't bother setting any guidelines as to who would get the axe. Forget qualifications. [Charles]was going to do it his way. How's that for democracy? If you want a dictator, [Charles's] your man. If you want quality education, it's time to vote for it.

Spot #4:
Some people say [Charles]'s a leader. Others claim he's a nitpicker. And a fair number call him an obstructionist. It's all a matter of opinion. We think

[Charles] is sincere in his beliefs but miserably short-sighted in his thinking. Instead of concentrating on the best possible education for Tyrone students, [Charles]seems more interested in his own personal agenda. That's no good if the students have to pay the price. What's your opinion?

One of the more effective print ads generated by the Stovers' Network of Concerned Citizens appeared in the May 30, 1992 *Tyrone Daily Herald*. It pointed out how the censorship coalition hypocritically ran for office on a platform of openness and individual expression but operated under a regime of deception and almost cartoonish unanimity:

[TOM and JULIE] PROMISED:

1. No secrets.
2. To establish joint committees of school board members and teachers for curriculum and education.
3. To reduce the insulation that exists between the teachers, administration, and board members.
4. An hour set aside before **EACH** meeting of the Board where the board will be accessible to the general public to **DISCUSS** any problems, not just to allow a few brief comments and ignore them.

Now Board members [Tom and Julie] have broken all these promises. They have acted to **WASTE MONEY AND HURT EDUCATION**.

But do they feel **SHEEPISH?**
HA!! They are **PROUD** of their deception. The **SHEEP** are right behind them, just watch and listen!
[Arthur]: **AYE, AYE, AYE, AYE**
[Charles]: **AYE, AYE, AYE, AYE**
[Dave]: **AYE, AYE, AYE, AYE**
Join us at the 7PM, June 9, TASD School Board Meeting

Eventually, the attack ads gained enough critical mass that Rick Reeves, Vice-President/General Manager of the local CBS affiliate WTAJ-TV, launched this multi-pronged diatribe against the censorship coalition. Reeves delivered perhaps the most lethal of political blows, as the April 1992 message was broadcast multiple times across a relatively large audience—all of central Pennsylvania:

> As demonstrated recently in Tyrone, electing school board directors can be a voter's most dangerous task. Congressional candidates who may be entertaining but not too bright can, at least, be cancelled out by others of equal ability on the other side of the aisle.
>
> But a school board director with a partisan agenda, a political or God forbid a religious one, who has the limited awareness and unlimited arrogance, can effectively sentence school children to his own ignorance. Simply by denying access to information, the school board director can threaten the wellbeing of all the children in the system.
>
> School directors in Tyrone talk of sin while separating boys and girls in health and physical education classes, and some say they want no sex education in schools at all. No sex education when an AIDS epidemic is sweeping through the world? That's a painful example of what careless voting can do.
>
> There's another side to the damage, too. Students, certainly high school students, know that segregating boys and girls in those classes is a ridiculous pretense and withholding information about the health side of sex is irresponsible at best. Students will lose respect for the school board and the teachers and administrators who must follow it.
>
> We suspect the current problems with the Tyrone School Board are so blatant that the voters will correct them. But the same opportunities for disaster exist all over. Look closely when people run for school board. Make sure they're at least as smart as your kids to begin with.

Obviously, when free expression is under attack from the public, as it was in our schools in the 1990's, sometimes the best recourse is to plunder the free expression war chest and get the message out. Like it or not, political action—even in the form of the negative campaign advertisement—may be democracy's most effective medium for the message.

But when free expression is threatened from within the district, even by our own teachers, political savvy is also indispensable in finding resolution. In response to the Vietnam War effort, Tyrone students in the early 1970's published a peace symbol in the school newspaper *The Spokesman*. In more cosmopolitan locales, the peace symbol was by then passé, but the political upheaval of the 60's hit the Tyrone area a decade late. A Problems of Democracy teacher who was ultra-conservative in his rhetoric and politics called the peace symbol "communistic"— emblematic of the Black Panthers—and wanted district personnel to take disciplinary action against the students who published it. No action was taken to punish the students. In fact, I recall that a brilliantly vocal student, Virginia Smith[6], with a few others, boldly challenged the teacher in class when he screened films produced by the The John Birch Society.

The teacher was not pleased with what he perceived to be his independent-minded students' unchallenged free speech, however, and perhaps to drive his perspective home, he later introduced his class to a far-right leaning news article calling the works of Martin Luther King communistic. In fact, in an act that barred further discussion of King's leanings, the teacher constructed a "True/False" test with a question similar to: "*Martin Luther King is a communist.*" The answer, just to quell all doubt, was "*True.*" An African-American physician in town objected on several grounds, not least among them the several children he had in the district's schools. A meeting with the department chair was held and the teacher was required to seek department approval before introducing any further lopsided inflammatory works to his classes—a move that still allowed him the academic freedom to innovate but which reminded him that his job was to present both sides of an issue, not to indoctrinate students with propaganda. He was not pleased with these terms, and it became clear that dealing with him might present the expected minefields of union involvement and litigation.

---

6 Dr. Smith graduated with top honors from Bucknell and Penn State, became a professor at Penn State, and works presently as a Philadelphia educational entrepreneur.

Fortunately for us, he also dabbled in selling mutual funds as a financial advisor—this at a time when our teachers were compensated rather poorly. Fortuitously, his business must have prospered so well that he eventually requested a leave of absence without pay, I assumed to attend to his mutual fund operation. Administratively, we had every right to deny his request. It would have felt good to do so, especially given his brazen disregard for student expression. Politically, however, the best thing was to graciously grant his request, let him establish his success elsewhere full-time, and hope that he would resign, saving the district the hassle of taking steps to remove him. This is precisely what happened. So the wisest way to ensure free expression is not always to lead a spirited and proactive charge. Remember, the Families for Quality Education radio campaign against Charles was on my part a passive approach. The community fought that battle, and so I was wise in staying silent while the cannons fired. Sometimes, as in the case of this internal enemy of free expression, the best political tactic is the more passive one, allowing the problem to go away on its own terms.

At other times, staff members need stern reminders that their words have enormous financial and political consequences—far greater than they can ever imagine—when they decide that it is imperative to speak their minds. This was certainly true in the case of a high school civics teacher whose loose lips in the classroom could have left the district in financial ruin and, through an unforeseeable sequence of events, could have led to massive tax increases on residents. Troubled by a friend's inability to secure a business loan from Mid-State Bank for his local hardware store, the civics teacher exercised his first amendment rights by maligning Mid-State in his classes, questioning their integrity and insinuating that Mid-State Bank was complicit in the misfortunes that befell the Tyrone Area School District during the Devon crisis. His wholesale condemnation of the bank was political dynamite—especially since some of the students in his classes were the children of Mid-State Bank employees. The kids, of course, told their parents of their teacher's civics lesson tirade, and the parents undoubtedly told their managers. All of this jeopardized recovery of funds eviscerated when Black's Ponzi scheme imploded. A Mid-State settlement meant that the largest chunk of the loss would have been recouped. Additional distributions from bankruptcy trustees would still be pursued, and several other third party collections eventually would approach a 100% recovery. It seemed a tough enough nut to crack even without further complications.

And then came the call from Mike Betts, our attorney in Pittsburgh, who said that he had just fielded a call from Washington, D.C.—from the attorney representing Mid-State Bank.

"Unfortunate news," he said, "One of your teachers is making comments in his class about Mid-State . . . he's really creating some significant issues. It could blow a really nice payoff."

Immediately, I approached the teacher in the presence of both the assistant principal and the principal. He fully disclosed his motives, that his friend in Bellwood had eventually lost his once-thriving hardware business when the bank had turned him down for any type of loan. I promptly wrote an apology that the civics instructor was required to read orally to each class under the supervision of the vice-principal. I informed Mike Betts of this action, which he concurred would be a wise measure.

We never heard another word from Mid-State.

The lesson, of course, is that free expression is not always free, especially when it is irresponsible. There are huge costs in abusing our first amendment rights. Our civics teacher was not necessarily yelling "fire!" in a crowded theatre, but he was setting off smoke bombs in frustration, "venting"—a volatile form of free expression in any work place. Eventually, when the smoke cleared, we recovered all funds plus most attorney fees. Our legal counsel informed us that the probability of such an outcome was virtually "unheard of" in the realm of Ponzi scheme settlements—perhaps a one in a thousand shot.

I'm told that a Rubik's cube has 43 quadrillion combinations, so its solution obviously requires some combination of intellect and persistence. While our team possessed a fair dose of both, Vegas was not betting on us. As board member Reverend Norman Huff concluded, it was "something of a miracle," and since Norman assured us that he prayed daily for us, I smiled and thanked him.

Some folks have difficulty wrapping their heads around the role of religious expression in public schools. As far as Reverend Huff and many of us were concerned, God's hand was on us throughout the Devon crisis. It was a spiritual as well as a fiscal challenge—with real spiritual growth for many of us. God was not only in our schools; Reverend Huff believed He had saved them. When we share this insight, some folks find it contradictory that we cannot allow free expression of religion at every school's most politicized venue—commencement. Our schools do as much as they can legally to support religious expression. Our students annually "Rally Around the Pole" to pray in the mornings. We have enjoyed student-directed religious music performances in the high school courtyard. Students and their churches have organized prayer and Bible study clubs over the years on district grounds. We proudly pronounce "under God" as we pledge the flag at the start of each school day and at school board meetings. We call our Christmas assemblies what they are, despite the competing presence of Kwanza, Ramadan, and Hanukkah—and Good Friday is still a day off. As in so many public schools, some of our best literature lessons are taught around Christian parables, Norse creation stories, or allusions to Talmud, Torah, and Koran. But when commencement season strikes, the American Civil Liberties Union (ACLU) is hyper-vigilant.

One commencement evening in 1994, we invited as commencement speaker honorable Judge Brooks Smith, a Tyrone alumnus who is currently judge in the 3rd Circuit Court of Appeals, to which he was elected in 2002. One of our two featured student speakers had drafted a prayer with problematic religious overtones, declaring Jesus Christ as "our savior" among other audience-inclusive Christian references that would certainly activate ACLU radar. The speech was laden with enough fervor and dogma that it would not be constitutionally permitted in a public school under separation of church and state precedents. The student was urged to redraft and "tone down" the piece. He did not refuse and gave the full impression that he would comply. So to the best of our knowledge, he dutifully revised the address under the tutelage of the speech coach, who was particularly well-versed in Christian theology and more than capable of suggesting constitutional ways to express faith in a wise and caring Creator.

But all of our precaution was to no avail. When the student got on stage, he commanded the venue like a martyr and forged ahead, apparently with the original script. Of course, there was a small part of me that admired the student's resolve, but my oath of allegiance as a superintendent is to uphold the Constitution, and to defend the Commonwealth—including the taxpayer, who can be on the hook for tens of millions of dollars when heady students confuse a podium for a pulpit. Today, kids like this are YouTube heroes in their home towns—until the ACLU arrives with the lawsuit. Then what looked like courage under dim commencement lights looks more like defiance or idiocy. This particular student flouted his independence from us and from the law of the land. It was rumored that he would return to his original script at the commencement exercise and to see it through. In his mind, perhaps he was an afflicted Apostle Paul, and we the heartless Romans hell-bent on his persecution.

This was high school Principal Neil Smith's last commencement as he retired that year. I had invited staff who had participated in commencement exercises to my home that evening for refreshments. Judge Smith was there with his wife, and he mentioned to me that he had just made the decision on the bench that what the student had done had violated the law of the land. My reaction may be hard for some to understand, but it was my job to uphold the constitutional rights of all within the schools. Doing so does not win anybody a popularity contest. I hung my head. I was ashamed of what had happened and accepted responsibility for my oversight. The prospect has haunted me ever since that in the wrong hands the district could have been sued over the incident. It was not the last such episode.

Another incident occurred later when a local business leader was our commencement speaker. It should be noted that we had invited Christian ministers to speak at our commencement ceremonies on previous occasions, one especially by the name of Roger Wagner from an Altoona church. Wagner, like so many secular speakers through the years, was able to convey powerful Christian messages to our grads without excluding other religious groups or showing favor to one particular denomination. Still, the business leader persisted in making numerous specific and unveiled references to Jesus Christ, again in defiance of the Constitution. Perhaps he was unaware of the unconstitutionality of his statements. Thereafter, Principal Tom Yoder and I met and decided that in the future we would review all speeches that were to be given at commencement—not just student speeches.

Lest critics assail us for being spiritually timid in making this policy call, it was less than two days after this businessman's speech that two women came to see Tom Yoder in his office. They were deeply aggrieved that the speaker had made so many Christian-specific comments during commencement at the exclusion of other faiths. We were thankful that they had chosen to visit us first rather than their local chapter of the ACLU—and they were thankful that prior to their meeting Tom and I had already implemented a means to prevent a future breech of the Constitution.

On a few other occasions, our efforts to foster free expression among students became politicized. During the 2010 and 2011 school years, a student pep group emerged that challenged the limits of free expression at athletic events. Several of the students, some of them athletes and members of the state-runner-up football team of 2011, formed a group that many considered a notoriously wild and abrasive entity; they called themselves the

"Dawg Pound." Many of these participants and their parents were concurrently dismayed that Coach Franco would be making an exodus to Altoona and that the board and administration were not doing all that they could to retain him.

As the antics of the Dawg Pound became more offensive, the necessity to leash and muzzle some of their behaviors intensified. A Dawg Pounder at various sporting events dressed up like a Mexican replete with super-sized sombrero, black mustache, and poncho. One of the Pound Parents relished the humor and video-taped his act to post on YouTube, although they were advised by the district not to do so. Eventually, more brazen videos were posted, some showing the parents of opposing teams reportedly expressing open irritation toward Dawg Pounders who reportedly taunted them in the lobby at intermission and ridiculed their kids on the court with insulting nicknames. Once, members of the Pound dubbed a long-haired player from Bald Eagle Area "Pony Boy," inciting his father to near physical hostility. These parents protested when students were chastised for such chants, saying that the students were only trying to have fun. These behaviors reached their dark depths of name-calling and bullying when, at a game with Central Mountain, the school where Jerry Sandusky had coached and groomed one of his abuse victims, the Dawg Pound shouted in unison, "You just got Sanduskied" whenever our team made a basket.

Such blatant lack of respect could warrant suspensions. Administration met with the parents who were unhappy with our stance, but the parents (some of them Franco football supporters) were blind to the unsportsmanlike conduct of their kids, com-plaining that surrounding school districts had Dawg Pound groups whom they believed were far more aggressive and inappropriate. Some walked out of the meetings. Meanwhile, we bolstered security at athletic events, made immediate changes and clarifications in the *Student Handbook*, prohibited costumes at events, and required a school-appointed administrator or officer to sit with the Dawg Pound at every sporting event—even the away ones.

Still, several parents tried to pit the community against the administration in the matter. Those parents and students interpreted the lack of support for such cheering as a lack of support for athletics and students in general—and especially for Coach Franco. During the football season, Franco had sent emails to the administration expressing dissatisfaction with several managerial decisions by the dean of students and principal regarding the discipline of his players. He claimed that he would discipline his players far more severely than the school would do. Earlier in the year, he claimed he would be much harder in practice on rule-breaking players than the school could be in a detention hall or suspension room setting. Several Dawg Pound members instigated informal spontaneous protests in the school cafeteria during lunch, apparently chanting to voice their independence or displeasure. Afterwards, they paraded down the high school hallway while students were taking required state examinations and chanted "U.S.A., U.S.A.!"—perhaps not as a patriotic expression but simply to defy the freedom-denying dean and principal, whom they most likely believed were to blame for squelching the Pound.

Nonetheless, I re-committed myself that year to encouraging free expression for kids—just as I had done for over a decade—with a senior survey of the class of 2012. I have said before that part of free expression is a full willingness to hear what you do not want to hear, but it is also an opportunity to hear what is going well and to assess long-range goals and future action. In the wake of the Dawg Pound and Franco's declared exit, I suspected that the senior interviews in 2012 would serve up anything but milquetoast. Prior to 2008, I had always invited a representative group of students to sit down with me a month or so prior to graduation to chat about their experiences in the district. I would chart their responses to key questions that served as barometers of effectiveness: how safe do you feel at school, how interesting are classes, how fairly are rules enforced, how well do students and teachers treat each other with respect? I would also invite open-ended responses about what they would change in the school or what teachers they most valued. I valued these student expressions of opinion so much that since 2001, I had used their feedback almost exclusively to reward staff as "Distinguished Educators" with $1,000 checks from an anonymous donor.

I experienced with this survey some extremely uplifting and validating moments. One student pointed out that our art teacher was "the funniest teacher at TAHS and does his job wonderfully . . . Everyone takes advantage of his kind heart that is willing to do anything for anyone and takes on way too many jobs, but always gets them done with precision." Another student praised our metal shop instructor: "He taught me so many life lessons . . . He was like a father to me in high school. I will never forget that man." One junior English teacher drew the adulation of more students than any other teacher on staff, for he had earned a reputation as one who would help students who were not even assigned to his roster: "He encouraged me to do better . . . and believed that I could do better as a student in his class. He even helped me my sophomore year when [my teacher] did not explain her teachings or what she wanted from our writings or work."

These students did not tell us just what we wanted to hear; they were respectfully critical, asking that we focus more on SAT preparation, for example, and less on PSSA preparation. We took their advice, ramping up SAT skills in English and increasing vocabulary lists from 5 words per week to 25 words—a 500% increase in Honors classes. We tied SAT grammatical skills and reading skills in with our current instruction and evaluation instruments. We also started making the PSAT mandatory for all non-IEP students. The results were measurable. In just one year, SAT Reading scores increased 20 points, while the national average was virtually unchanged.

But some of the opinions voiced by the Class of 2012 read like red graffiti sprayed on a restroom wall. They reflected anger over a lost football coach, of course, but also the misplaced values of a small clique of parents and citizens, who not only condoned the students' lack of respect but posted it on social networking sites and on YouTube as perverse sources of amusement and pride. These brazen displays of disrespect—for their community, for their guests, for their school, for themselves—may have led these students to make anonymous comments like these:

> **Q:** Which high school staff member impacted most positively upon your high school days?
> **A:** Coach John Franco. He might not be a teacher here but obviously he's not a coach here anymore, whoever had any say in that is a [f-----] dumbass I don't care what anyone says about how the school couldn't have kept him . . . you're losing money getting rid of him, idiots. We'll see what happens to this school in the next couple years, it's gonna go to [sh-t] because of [f-----] fags . . .

> **Q:** What would you recommend to improve our school system?
> **A:** Well first, fire everyone from the school board. They're all greedy [pr-cks] and care about nothing but themselves. They say they care about the kids and their education but they are full of [sh-t] . . .

While these students' words represented a minority of student responses, they also represented a reshuffling of the deck regarding the methodology by which we solicited student feedback. While their words were as harsh as they were vacant, they needed to be heard, for inviting free expression is the greatest sign of respect. As soon as we undervalue respect in either a personal, professional, or political relationship, we accelerate the half-life of that relationship

To further illustrate the importance of encouraging an atmosphere of free expression and respect for others and what they have to offer to the health of relationships in an institution; I would be remiss in closing this lesson if I did not reflect on those who at one juncture or another may have felt that I disrespected them and what I then did as attempted compensation. I think of Carla Ruscio, a former board secretary who was once disgruntled about her son's education and was awarded 153 hours of compensation time in a settlement as approved by the hearing officer. The Department of Education granted approval for Mrs. Ruscioto use that time to tutor her son for his SATs—and he eventually graduated from Penn State. Later, after she left the district, she sent me an email to tell me how much she valued her time here. I think of an angry Penny Stroup, whose son suffered multiple disabilities and protested what she deemed the "outrageous" conditions of our facilities. We eventually remedied those conditions within our consolidated building program. I thought that it was a practical joke when a bouquet of flowers arrived in my office in June of 2013 at my retirement. When I saw Penny Stroup's and her son's name on the card, I was so incredulous that I called the florist to verify the sender. Then I called Penny and thanked her personally for the flowers. Over the years, others who at the time were unhappy with our decisions often have acknowledged our efforts on behalf of their children. At times administrators went out of their way to recommend hiring folks who we suspected were disrespected for all the wrong reasons. I think of Mr. Rossman, without question one of the most effective special education teachers in the history of our schools. Not many employers would have shown him respect in the hiring process because he had worked as a custodian for ten years before earning his teaching certificate. He had received a DUI which had delayed his graduation from college. In his application material he provided a genuine response to explain his situation. What a loss it would have been for our students had mutual respect not been the cornerstone of our working relationship. His class, comprised mostly of non-itinerant special education kids, cooked us Thanksgiving and Christmas dinner every year in his facility, using the life skills that Mr. Rossman had taught them. How proud they were to explain to all of us what ingredients went into each meal and how they had prepared it.

This is what respect looks like—an email from a formerly irritated employee, a bouquet from an old critic, a chance at success for someone whose value others cannot see. On several occasions I overstepped my own standards of respect—one very close to my retirement, when I raised my voice in a conference call with a concerned citizen who had been frequenting board meetings in the wake of the Dawg Pound fray and the Franco departure. Some suspected that he was really present at meetings as part of a concern to "bring back Franco" (a prospect which incidentally I neither count nor discount). In frustration over an issue that is now so trivial I cannot recall it, I did raise my voice. Lest you believe such an isolated lapse of respect has no consequence, especially for a superintendent of forty-odd years who might feel invulnerable to the fall-out of a simple voice-raising, consider that the month after my retirement I received in my home mailbox a confidential letter from the Governor's Office of General Counsel. Assistant Counsel Shane F. Crosby directed the letter to notify me of a formal professional educator complaint alleging that I had "acted unprofessionally in a conference call by raising your voice and yelling at the complainant." Thank goodness I could not be fired. But it is a lesson in respect that every educator must heed.

As for the Dawg Pounders and some of their cheeky commentators from the Class of 2012, I would not have started inviting their commentary over a decade ago if I did not consider it indispensable to the success of our schools. I did so out of respect for them. Sometimes these are not the types of words we want to hear from the mouths of babes, of course. But I don't condemn them.

Babes just repeat what they hear at home.

Principles of Prevailing

- ✓ Elicit free expression . . . to do anything less is ethically, administratively, and politically dangerous—even if the words we hear are hard to listen to.
- ✓ The politically expedient course of action in censorship attempts is to squelch the controversial materials; do not choose expedience over principle.

✓ The basis of many religions—and of our government—is freedom of choice. Do not legislate morality—nor allow others to do the same.

✓ The wisest way to ensure free expression is not always to lead a spirited and proactive charge. To a degree, use a passive approach. The community will fight the battle.

✓ Invite kids to speak; survey them personally. Their words will speak loudest.

✓ Beware of commencement.

"First thing we do, let's kill all the lawyers."
—William Shakespeare
(*2 Henry VI*, 4.2.59), Dick the Butcher to Jack Cade

8 | "Kill" a Lawyer,
And Other Ways to Save a Buck

When Shakespeare's Dick the Butcher advocated killing lawyers in *Henry VI*, one can imagine how heartily Elizabethan audiences howled. Perhaps it was a cheap shot even then, but there is little doubt that butcher and barrister alike smirked. The lawyer joke has resonated over the centuries, which is why a wise superintendent will intercept the punch line and minimize the fees assessed by solicitors and subsidized by local taxpayers, as well as maximize the economic use of attorneys. "Other Ways" to maximize a buck include efficient cost savings, methods of financing, physical plant facilities, and other related savings[7].

Over the forty-two years of my superintendence, I quickly realized from the school board meetings I attended that it is not necessary to have an omnipresent attorney, though that is the usual practice for most if not all Blair County school boards and for those in other counties throughout the state. Most if not all other districts demand an attorney's presence as an unquestioned meeting fixture, when, in fact, such presence is necessary only on

---

7 Related savings such as requesting savings initiatives from all staff as well as suggestions from a cross section of citizen taxpayers based upon priorities of a concentric circle concept.

special occasions. Empowering qualified individuals from the board or from the administrative team can save a considerable amount of money. I am fairly certain that one reason boards demand legal omnipresence is that many of them make direct, personal connections with attorneys during the negotiations process (or some social connection) and later come to find them as indispensable as coffee-makers to the milieu of any meeting, despite the redundancy of knowledge and expertise at the table.

Not only did my predecessor and father Norman Miller embrace a hands-off approach to legal counsel, so did the school boards under which I served. My long-term assessment of the amount of money we saved Tyrone taxpayers by excluding attorneys runs into hundreds of thousands of dollars. If one is in a situation of continual turmoil, when legal issues erupt on a constant basis, then, of course, one must make legal allowances. For instance, when the Tyrone Area School District was involved in the Devon fraud case, a board-meeting attorney was occasionally present. In most situations, though, with members of the administration and the superintendents adhering to Roberts Rules of Order, to the Pennsylvania School Code, the Sunshine Law, and to arbitration decisions, meetings can proceed with sufficient legal background to handle questions that arise. With questions demanding legal advice, further independent research on the administrator's clock (rather than on the law firm's) can yield workable solutions and alternatives in future meetings.

Generally speaking, having the prescience to study the agenda well in advance and to predict what hot topics might be a-buzz in the mind of the community should guide the decision to involve a legal presence or not. If the agenda entails a bond issue or a special education case in closed session, one should make an attorney present. Occasionally, we asked lawyers to be present at public meetings if the issues were complex enough, as they were during the district's bout with censorship. Pennsylvania School Board Association (PSBA) Chief Counsel Stephen Russell advised those attending one of several public censorship meetings that "the personal beliefs of individuals, whether political, social, moral, or religious may not be used to justify the removal of school resources" and that only factors such as space, obsolescence, or "lack of educational suitability" may play a role in removal. His presence provided an invaluable educational backdrop for our hot-button censorship challenge. Still, for too many districts statewide, the standard operating procedure is that the attorney always attends. Once I mentioned to an administrator at a county-level meeting where an attorney was present that he could have easily fielded all of the legal questions by himself. He responded with a smile.

The same playbook should be implemented with contract negotiations, where an attorney's services are not only unnecessary but perhaps a subtle sign of either weakness or suspicion to both parties present. Pivotal to remember is that attorneys do not have to live with the outcomes of contracts—they merely facilitate their adoption. By relegating attorneys to minimal or inconsequential roles in bargaining, board members and administrators alike feel more accountable for the outcomes by which they must abide after the ink is dry.

I should add that never did the board conduct a formal teacher dismissal hearing or an arbitration case in the presence of a lawyer, and only one student expulsion ever required an attorney's assistance. Such situations can be particularly volatile, of course. Staff members had always been offered the presence of an attorney but unilaterally declined a formal hearing before the board with legal representation, most likely choosing an alternative career pathway instead of retaliation or vindication. Special education hearings, on the other hand, require the presence of an attorney, and for fact-finding purposes we used the services of PSBA's Dave Devare for a nominal fee—far less than an attorney would charge.

Another route that can be explored in the economical use of attorneys is to secure inexpensive services offered by PSBA for dues-paying members of the association. It is a free call to a Pennsylvania School Board Association solicitor to obtain some direct advice, not to represent the district but merely to obtain counsel that would have cost significant sums elsewhere. For decades until his retirement, the district's primary counsel through PSBA was Don Owen, whom I visited in his Harrisburg office, where I took notes from him on sensitive issues and was never charged a cent. More recently, we enlisted the services of Emily Leader and eventually Sean Fields, who was always a free phone call away. Of course, while face-time solicitations through PSBA attorneys are no longer free, they are still affordable, quick, and reliable. Thus, by knowing the school code intimately and by tapping legal resources sparingly, I estimate conservatively that we saved the Tyrone Area School District more than half of a million dollars over my tenure. A superintendent who knows the law well will save his district dearly—and a record of thrift will be his most valuable political advocate when he needs one the most—especially when taxes must be raised. The 2012-13 Pennsylvania equalized millage[8] table below from PDE.org illustrates the degree to which saving a penny here or there saved Tyrone residents dearly at tax time:

State Rank	School District, 2012-13	Equalized Mills
1	*Byrn Athyn SD*	*1.3*
2	Windber Area SD	7.6
3	Turkeyfoot Valley Area SD	8.2
4	Rockwood Area SD	8.3
5	Southern Huntingdon County SD	8.5
6	North Clarion County SD	9.1
7	Chestnut Ridge SD	9.5
8	Shanksville-Stonycreek SD	9.7
9	Tyrone Area SD	9.8
10	Fannett-Metal SD	9.8

Source: pde.org. September 13, 2013.

In the end, a superintendent owes nothing to the law but to follow it; in the process and used sparingly, lawyers can be valuable in helping a school district survive. The services of Mike Betts of Pittsburgh in particular were invaluable to seeing the district through its most trying moments like the Devon fraud case —as have been the advice and services of other school lawyers with whom we contracted over my tenure. Mike was a relentless master of the legal game, a tremendously adept and dedicated professional without whose help the district could not have recovered its funds. Choosing only the finest counsel and using them with discretion meant that Tyrone taxpayers and students under our watch could enjoy one of the state's best educational bargains.

Because saving on attorney fees was part of a thrift mindset that administrative teams and school boards modeled throughout my tenure, we had a large degree of control over the savings. When economic crises struck, however, the politics of saving became much more unwieldy. During the fiscal cliff crisis of 2011 and 2012, when Governor Corbett reduced funding to public education,

8 Equalized mills include all the local tax efforts (wage, property, head tax, etc) combined. This chart shows that Tyrone Area SD was one of the lowest local taxing effort of 500 districts in the state.

very few if any superintendents, from the wealthiest to the poorest districts, felt in control of savings. A perfect storm of retirement contribution spikes, expirations in federal funds, and a painfully slow economic recovery from the 2008 recession meant drastic changes and into-the-bone cuts to long cherished programs.

When that era of "radical efficiency" finally and recently dawned, we attempted to apply the same surgical fiscal restraint that we exercised with school board lawyers to every nook and cranny of the budget, although we found limited success in areas over which we did not have total authority. For example, in 2012, just before radical efficiency erupted on the public spectrum and Corbett indicated that there would be significant losses for Tyrone to the tune of a million dollars, initially there was not extensive discussion by superintendents about budget cutbacks—largely because federal funds were granted to the state. The state used this money freely to lavish on public schools in lieu of regular state subsidies. There should have been more murmurings of concern—and there were some expressed by Superintendent Dennis Murray and superintendents in Blair County and through-out the state. Perhaps as a group, local superintendents could have been more politically aggressive on the issue. Whereas the basic education allotment had been bolstered by one-time federal dollars, perhaps schools spent those dollars as if they were allocated for repeated costs like new programs and positions. Alas, when the federal funding was no longer available—when we had arrived at federal "sequestration," or what many others called the fiscal cliff, the funding dried up from the state.

Although many folks perceived me as the fiscal personification of Chicken Little, I had approached the director of the IU, whom I admire and respect, about his budget and stated that he had a significant surplus. Because we would be basing our IU contributions based on WADM's and (AR)[9] aid ratios, I suggested to the executive director that we eliminate our local contribution of $6,000. The amount for all member districts combined approached $173,000. Decades earlier through the transfer of entities enact-ment, we transferred all of our IU classes into our district, saving hundreds of thousands of dollars. Furthermore, the teachers we hired were much more affordable, giving credit for their salary step without the heftier salaries that the IU had paid for the identical step. More recently, we pooled our preschool transportation contract from the IU, which according to an analysis conducted by Cathy Harlow cut the cost of bus runs in half.

---

9 A reflection of the wealth of a district in the state, and the higher the aid ratio the poorer the district.

The IU director thanked me for my input. I said, "Well, being professional, I'm going to let you know that I am going to bring up this point before the IU budget is voted on by the super-intendents." I told him that I felt very strongly that we needed to tighten the belt in preparation for the loss of state and federal funding. I proceeded to make such comments to all of the super-intendents. I reiterated that we needed to address the possible future financial nightmare that was headed our way and needed to prioritize, conserve, and reduce all aspects of expenditures where possible. At the time, mine was a voice of doom and gloom that perhaps few others wanted to hear.

After having my say, some discussion followed. There was a motion and a vote: the budget was passed as usual with all of the districts paying their customary local share. Tyrone's was the only voice in the wilderness that day voting against the proposed IU budget. Chicken Little had come home to roost. I share this to illustrate how little control a superintendent has at times when it comes to district finances. All of my maneuvering with regard to IU funding was for naught. Still, understanding both the voice of the majority and the finance committee's recommendation of the budget for approval, I made my strong admonitions about the looming fiscal cliff.

Lo and behold, it was not long before the fiscal cliff emerged before us, ushering in an era that would spell a sweeping down-sizing of our in-house vocational program- a potential political firestorm if not handled judiciously. For years we had attempted to contain the spiraling unsustainability of the vocational wing. Tyrone at that time housed one of the most comprehensive academic and vocational high schools left in Pennsylvania. Of course, most schools long ago began to bus their students to regional Career and Technology Centers—as had nearly all Blair County high schools, except Tyrone. Tyrone's distinction as a "comprehensive" high school was a source of deep vocational and historical pride, particularly in a blue-collar community that was heavily represented in World War II, when military success hinged on the vocations.

After the vocational department had served the country in wartime, the postwar moment had now become serviced to the community of Tyrone. The department enhanced its visibility in the school by serving banquets, opening a school cafeteria, building classroom bookshelves and cupboards, and repairing school and home electrical equipment. In home economics, car-pentry, electronics, and numerous other career classes, vocational education had enhanced its visibility. As vocational visibility increased, so did versatility, especially in the realms of electronics, agriculture, and carpentry. Under the leadership of electronics instructor Edward Thomas, students completed the wiring of the first public address system in the history of the district. By 1957, under the leadership of novice carpentry teacher Robert Westley, Tyrone's carpentry students built miniature scale models of actual houses. By 1964, on land across from Tyrone's 1961 high school, homes were constructed for eventual sale to Tyrone residents.

It was against this backdrop of entrenched vocational success and pride that the fiscal realities of 2011 seemed so ominous. In the wake of our fiscal decisions with the IU over the decades, we decided that three political survival strategies were paramount: ramped up public relations, total transparency, and direct community involvement. Yet we were not naïve; we knew that in the end, despite all of our best efforts to save money in a time of crisis, by involving the community in this emotionally-entrenched area of curriculum, we were surrendering a degree of power and authority—a surrender which might mean that we would save no money at all—and perhaps pay more. We knew that we had to let the others at the table to understand the best way to save; but other players would also have their own agendas, some filled with ancillary concerns that were neither fiscal nor curricular in scope.

Toward this end, we tapped the public relations acumen of long-time English teacher Richard Merryman to help present the inevitable vocational cuts to the community in the best possible light through a series of articles in *TyNotes*, a regular newsletter to the community about our schools. In a 2011 edition of *TyNotes*, Merryman's sensitivity to the military community and to the many community donors who had supported the program over the decades was indispensable.

Merryman's rhetorical packaging of the vocational cut-backs as a "new day" in *TyNotes* helped calm what might have been more turgid political waters. Fiscally speaking, Merryman's focus on dwindling enrollment was paramount. In 1964, the year that Robert Westley embarked on Tyrone High's first home building mission, the enrollment stood at 3,411. In 1976, when Tyrone school administrators petitioned the Pennsylvania Board of Education to certify Tyrone High as an official vocational school within the walls of Tyrone's comprehensive high school, the student population held steady at 3,151. (Incidentally, the Pennsylvania Board of Education denied that petition—probably because a larger, more encompassing vocational school already existed in nearby Altoona.) By 2011, in contrast, K-12 enrollment was at its nadir—approximately 1,800 students, or 2,000 students with pre-K included.

As we pointed out in *TyNotes as* a matter of fiscal transparency, "The mathematics of this involves simple subtraction: the district has lost [over 1,000] students since Westley began his vocational home building mission in 1964 . . . And for those folks who still struggle with this condition, there is an even simpler way to describe it—when a district loses students, it loses state funding, and rarely can the state funding shortfall be recovered by increasing property taxes." However, the same funding formula has not been followed for a number of years in relationship to enrollment. Districts like Tyrone's—which have lost enrollment – will suffer only under future legislation, which will serve larger pieces of the fiscal pie to growing districts.

Eventually, the school's vocational environment would deteriorate. We lacked the financial resources to support a diversified vocational curriculum. Some programs had already reached a point where some individual class sections contained as few as five students. Whether we liked it or not, the board gradually discontinued auto mechanics, drafting, electronics, law enforcement, machining, and fine woodworking. Consider that for a modern public school to maintain an independent auto shop, we needed: a diagnostic analyzer at $6,500; an all-data systems subscription at $3,500 each year; basic hand tools costing about $4,000. Add to this nearly $15,000 for equipment another $70,000 in total compensation for a seasoned instructor, all for a vocational shop that might enroll twelve students.

Another painful vocational budget-cutting focus related to the school's long-established home-building mission. In 1964, when Westley pioneered vocational home-building at Tyrone, he insisted that the project involve all shops.

"These days," lamented Business Administrator Cathy Harlow in a *TyNotes* piece, "Tyrone lacks sufficient vocational shops to become intimately involved in any house project. Consequently, as Tyrone High's last house building mission unfolded, the district had to subcontract too many dimensions of the work to outside vendors: excavating, masonry, electrical, drywall, heating and air conditioning, plumbing, and carpeting. The cost to the district to employ those seven outside contractors totaled $84,783." The really depressing part, Harlow added, is that "because of scheduling constraints, our students could not even be present to observe and learn from the subcontracted professionals as they accomplished their designated tasks. So once again, Tyrone students suffered." Harlow explained that dwindling vocational opportunities at Tyrone High had accounted for the increase in our vocational student enrollment at The Greater Altoona Career and Technology Center (GACTC).

When Harlow had arrived as business administrator in 1994, few local students had been enrolled in the Altoona vocational center. Seventeen years later in 2011, Tyrone High had twenty-three high school students attending GACTC for half of their school day. Of course, attending GACTC also spelled higher costs for the school district. For each Tyrone student attending GACTC, Tyrone School District had to pay about $6,000 in yearly tuition. If the Tyrone School District became an official sponsor or member, as had the Bellwood School District, the yearly tuition quite possibly might decrease to $4,000 per student.

While we had closed more vocational classes in the past ten years than remained open in the present school, we emphasized that the collapse of our vocational classes had nothing to do with the competence of our class instructors. At the verge of the fiscal cliff, only six career-oriented programs remained: accounting technologies, agricultural production, carpentry, cooperative education, production industries technologies, and nursing.

As Merryman had underscored for the community the advantages of the GACTC over our own facilities and programs in a tactful way, he also highlighted how few enhancement opportunities remained within the district as opposed to the plethora of enhancements in the program available in nearby Altoona. In contrast to our six offerings, GACTC offered twenty-six career areas; more modern equipment; a much larger budget; licensing capacities that allowed the technical institution to certify competent students for the Middle States College Association or for business and industry; job apprenticeship opportunities with eventual career and job placement; and advanced placement potential in the practical nursing program, whereby nursing schools such as Penn State Altoona's and Mount Aloysius' would award advanced placement credits for hours clocked in the practical nursing program. Plus, GACTC offered yearly scholarships for high school seniors in each of the twenty-six programs, totaling almost $60,000 in annual assistance.

Still, Merryman did not sugar-coat the shortcomings of the GACTC experience. He indicated that school board members would "prove themselves extremely naïve and shortsighted" if they failed to recognize the entanglements. As it stood, Tyrone schools still would need to pay close to $4,000 per school year for each student who had elected to attend GACTC. If the school board ultimately voted to align itself with GACTC, all Tyrone students who chose an occupational major at the center would spend four consecutive periods a day (either all morning or all afternoon) taking training in Altoona. Thus, there would emerge a trio of entanglements: tuition, a split school day, and transportation— and all three ultimately did combine to derail the savings that our district might have realized in the vocational restructuring. In addition, as in every county school, some students who hoped to enroll at GACTC might not qualify for a given Altoona-based program. Consequently, even though our board members might elect to participate in GACTC, they still would need to maintain at least some practical foundation courses in the home school for those students unable or unwilling to attend at Altoona.

I announced that should the board decide to align itself with the Greater Altoona Career and Technology Center, Tyrone High would retain scaled down vocational areas in accounting/business, cooperative education, agricultural science, carpentry, nursing, and some version of combined metal/wood-working/home main-tenance. At Tyrone High, these six occupational classes would act as a core foundation for those students who chose not to or could not attend the Greater Altoona Career and Technology Center. In addition, Tyrone students might elect to enroll in one of these three classes for merely one period per day as an elective class, in which they could enhance skills they might need to function economically and effectively in the households of the future. Thus, Tyrone High's future approach to vocational education would hopefully retain adequate possibilities and attractive flexibility for those Tyrone students whose career path did not lead them to half-day enrollment at the Greater Altoona Career and Technology Center.

If we were to save significant funds, though, our program had to limit itself to staffing only these six occupational areas. Despite enflamed community emotions about the proposal, Cathy Harlow and I offered this caveat: "Some Tyrone citizens have the natural impression that the Tyrone Area School Board plans to decrease local vocational offerings simply to save money—this is untrue. The uncertain reality about this upcoming school board research is that we cannot be certain if our potential decision to transfer some occupational majors from Tyrone High to GACTC actually would save any money in the long run." In the end, all of our kids enjoy increased enhancements and opportunities with the GACTC alliance as well as with the six in-house programs that we had envisioned. The decision did nothing, however, to assuage the economic cuts that would have to be made when we met the fiscal cliff; it actually increased our expenditures.

We prepared the community for that reality with a three-part *TyNotes* edition to facilitate total transparency in this process. We referenced the new era of fiscal reality and subsequently produced a series of newspaper articles as well, articulating the financial and educational challenges confronting the district: that the governor's proposed budget reflected a reduction in state and federal funding of $1,677,544. With an anticipated increase of $1,000,000 in expenditures for the 2011-2012 year, the school district would face a potential $2,700,000 deficit.

The Tyrone Area School Board agreed to form a focus group consisting of fifteen district residents, including a high school student, who would interact with Business Administrator Cathy Harlow, with Director of Curriculum and Instruction Leslie Estep, and with me to share ideas addressing these issues. The focus group acted as communicators to the public. The group utilized a priorities-based concentric circle model to address a sweeping reduction in expenditures slated for the 2011-2012 school term at $1,708,248. The projected deficit would be offset with a proposed tax increase of approximately $260,500 while tapping a portion of the fund balance. The focus group understood that the era of fiscal reality was not a one-year phenomenon but a new challenge to do more with less. The concentric circle model would mean cuts to athletics and transportation before progressing to administrative specialists. Soon the cuts would affect custodians and librarians before they hit the classrooms, with teachers and students most directly affected.

Exacerbating the cutting was Governor Corbett's philosophy to support vouchers and school choice through Senate Bill 1[10], the nation's most aggressive approach in support of school choice. We were facing the most pressing survival situation ever for the public school system as we recognized it. The Pittsburgh law office of Ira Weiss stated that Governor Corbett's proposed budget included unprecedented cuts in both basic education subsidies and in key programs such as the accountability block grants which many school districts used to fund pre-K and after school programs. This combination of factors created the very real possibility that public education would be significantly marginalized in Pennsylvania.

Politically, we had no choice but to highlight in our public relations efforts the thrift that we practiced over the previous

---

10 Senate Bill 1 promised vouchers to attend all schools, including parochial. This money would be taken from the state reimbursement of the public school of residence of the student. Poorer districts would suffer greater negative economic impact as explained and demonstrated late in this lesson.

decades, which was the only silver lining in that dark cloud. In particular, we underscored the long-term planning of both current school board members and former members of decades ago, of school administration, and of the Tyrone community who had supported the consolidation and closing of the seven elementary schools (three schools in the 1970-1980s and four in the 1990s) into the eventual 1999 concept of one new elementary school, the addition of the middle school (Grades 5-8), and renovation of the high school (Grades 9-12). These decisions addressed the issue of equal opportunity for all of our school children. It was indispensable to our political survival during these recent and lean times that over the previous decades we had saved millions of dollars in our aggressive approach to internal consolidation. Likewise, we had provided monies through a planned Capital Reserve Fund over the decades to assist the district with the fiscal costs related to these building projects. The savings from the multiplicity of projects detailed below eclipsed the multi-millions—primarily because we paid off our debts far ahead of schedule—all $42,029,700 principal (plus any interest) in fourteen short years.

Capital Projects	Savings From Financial Physical Plant	Principal
1999	Pre-K to 4 Elementary School Project: 120,230 square feet	$13,500,000
1999	Renovated High School and New Middle School Addition: 221,845 square feet	$12,000,000
1999	Harry Sickler Athletic Field Complex [2 baseball fields, 2 softball fields, and a practice football/soccer field]: 35 acres	$1,500,000
2001	Renovated football stadium at Gray-Veteran's Memorial Field	$1,800,000
2003	Expansion to Middle School: added 59,000 square feet for a total of 221,845 square feet	$10,000,000
2004	Track and Field areas updated and renovated with adjacent stream banks reinforced and cleared	$325,000
2009	Installation of new HVAC systems to provide AC and a new energy efficient heating system to the new Middle School and High School buildings	$2,904,700
1999 to 2013	Total debt paid off in August 2013 in less than 14 years, saving taxpayers millions of dollars in interest	$42,029,700

From the 1990's, Business Administrator Cathy Harlow had been instrumental in managing the budget, and between 2008-2011 had interacted daily with me in every aspect of school administration as we continued to address the financial crisis. I reminded the public that Tyrone Area School District millage rates continued to be among the lowest in the state while its staff continued to provide a high quality educational program. This quality education was reflected in test scores and other measurements, as well as evident in the excellence of our arts and athletic programs. Yet there were still many other, unavoidable painful cuts to make—ones that would cost jobs and programs. Aside from the Devon debacle, the fiscal cliff was the most critical crisis we had faced.

However, we were still in much better shape than so many other districts because we had summoned the courage and commitment to do both the big and the little things right and to live within our means. The same penny-wise thrift that recently prompted us to question our IU contributions, perceived as Chicken Little economic posturing by some, propelled us to avoid our becoming pound-foolish. Such parsimony was nothing new. Decades earlier we had transferred special and gifted education services from the IU to our schools, saving hundreds of thousands of taxpayer dollars. Instead of losing track of the big picture, we innovated as well as economized without hurting instructional quality. We cut a $5,000 fitness coach position, but we sought organizational sponsorship from Albemarle, the Tyrone Elks Club, and other willing local businesses to restore the funding so that our kids could stay fit. In fact, the district's fitness facility usage burgeoned under the new program, with over 140 total users in some months, a 500% increase over the pre-cliff levels.

Vocational programs were also cut, but students enjoyed expansive options at the GACTC while retaining choices in house. As with the fitness program, our enrollment in some in-house vocational programs flourished exponentially post-fiscal cliff. A pioneering new-hire resuscitated our community-treasured agriculture curriculum and recruited students until enrollment exploded from a handful of students to over a hundred within a couple years. In December 2010, we generated an e-mail asking all district personnel to offer suggestions for saving money, regardless of the significance of the savings. The endeavor produced twelve typed pages of efficiencies, from eliminating classroom printers and setting all centralized district printers to gray-scale, to knocking down the temperature in the buildings from 71 to 69 degrees—a move that generated $17,000 in savings per year for each degree. Metal halide lighting fixtures bowed to high-output fluorescents. A half-century old gas-powered steam heating system with sieve-like branch lines surrendered to a lean and robust one that saved $93,500 a year. We cut a half-time band instructor, but the band broke decades-old competition scoring records and placed first in its class in the state. An early retirement incentive reaped savings at the top ends of our salary scales and sowed some of those dollars in fertile ground for a few new-hires at lower wage rates.

The cyber schools continued to bleed us, but we reenergized our effort to recruit students and to enhance our own in-house cyber school. We attempted unsuccessfully to court our students away from PA Cyber, our greatest cyber competitor, at the same time that in one year 100% of our high school cyber students scored proficient on their PSSA reading and writing exams. In contrast, the fifty Tyrone students enrolled in cyber-charter schools outside of our district were attending eleven different institutions that eventually all failed to make adequate yearly progress under No Child Left Behind. We continued to address these issues, improving our blended school offerings and striving toward optimum responsiveness to our students' needs.

When I reflect on this string of successes from my vantage point of a retired superintendent, I am almost surprised and thankful that we were able to do so much with so little. We cut 13% off the budget, yet academic, athletic, vocational, and artistic growth thumbed its nose at the change. Many public schools have enacted similar changes with similar strategies. No matter which metric we employed to measure our success, we exceeded expectations. While PVAAS (Pennsylvania Value Added Assessment System) rankings (which erase economic influences) placed our grads at the top of the state in academic growth in 2013, achievement rankings (which do not factor out the effects of wealth) from the *Pittsburgh Business Times* still placed Tyrone in the 85th percentile statewide—in 86th place out of 592 districts, ahead of many economically privileged LEA's (Local Educational Agency) within and outside the IU.

I originally entitled this book *The Politics of Survival*—as if survival were something to celebrate, like a tie in hockey or a proficient score on a test of basic skills. To great degree, the word *survive* detracts from the monumental efforts exerted by our staff, students, and community during these harshest of economic years. Tyroners have a legacy of toughness and resiliency. Local author and businessman Chuck Banas captured that legacy well in the title of a book chronicling the resiliency of the state-champion Tyrone football team in 1999: *Team, Toughness, Tyrone.* Undoubtedly, the community and schools of Tyrone did so much more than survive their fall from the fiscal cliff. Like a team galvanized by a cause, they prevailed.

Principles of Prevailing

- ✓ It is not necessary to have an omnipresent attorney as is the usual practice at board meetings.
- ✓ If one is in a situation of continual turmoil, when legal issues erupt on a constant basis, then, of course, one must make legal allowances.
- ✓ Study the agenda well in advance and predict what hot topics might be a-buzz in the mind of the community to guide the decision to involve legal presence.
- ✓ By relegating attorneys to minimal or inconsequential roles in bargaining, board members and administrators alike feel more accountable for the outcomes.
- ✓ Choosing only the finest counsel and using them with discretion means that taxpayers and students under your watch can enjoy the best educational bargain.
- ✓ Ask all district personnel to offer suggestions for saving money, regardless of the significance of the savings.
- ✓ Careful planning and financing of capital projects will reap significant savings for the tax payer.
- ✓ Elicit staff and community representatives in the process of saving resources.

"Politics have no relation to morals."
—Niccolo Machiavelli, author of *The Prince*

9 | Pester the Politicians

European democracy was still more ideological than actual in Machiavelli's age. It would take the tremors of revolution in the streets of Paris and the bold experiment in democracy in the states to see if politics could rise above the tactics Machiavelli observed in his seminal work *The Prince*. It is worth noting that Machiavelli did not actually endorse deception in politics—he merely described and documented how rulers governed. Deceit is a part of politics, as is feigning ignorance and refusing to address the full truth. Although it is difficult for me to do so, like Machiavelli, I will attempt in this lesson to make no moral judgments about politicians as I chronicle their stances on pivotal issues. They have a job to do, and they do it as they believe at the time their constituencies and financial supporters expect them to do it. To say that "politics has no relation to morals" does not mean that politicians are immoral, as the punch-lines about them so often suggest. The leaders whom I discuss here namely (Governor Corbett, Senator John Eichelberger, and others) are decent, hardworking, principled men who deserve respect.

Having said that, for their own survival Democratic lawmakers still focus on the voices that speak most loudly, or at least on those that can get closest to their ears. In legislative ears, money buys that access. This reality certainly explains why cyber educations CEOs like those of K12 Incorporated shower their largesse on political candidates eager to endorse legislation siphoning public dollars away from brick-and-mortar public schools, even from highly successful and competitive ones like Tyrone's and surrounding districts, and into their pockets. K12 Inc. contributed $824,802 to state campaigns across the country from 2004 through 2011, most of it money legally siphoned away from public schools in the form of tuition vouchers—but their operations were not always above-board. An FBI sting of Pennsylvania's largest cyber school led to the indictment of Pennsylvania Cyber Charter School's Nick Trombetta, whose mis-use of public funds spurred some politicians to start vacillating about tainted Trombetta-related campaign contributions. To their credit, Governor Tom Corbett's re-election committee felt compelled to return a $5,000 contribution made by Mr. Trombetta in December 2011. Corbett campaign manager Mike Barley said the governor had no relationship with the former cyber school boss. Still, even in the face of bottom-of-the-state test scores among Pennsylvania's cyber ranks, Corbett did the politically viable thing at the time and advanced cyber-friendly legislation at the expense of public schools.

Call me naïve or even foolish, but if one works from the principle that access to legislators' ears should not be bought, the superintendent's challenge is to gain access to legislators through organizations like PSBA (Pennsylvania School Board Association), PASA (Pennsylvania Association of School Administrators), PSEA (Pennsylvania State Education Association), and PARSS (Pennsylvania Association of Rural and Small Schools); through the press; through letter writing; through in-person meetings, or through more creative channels. However it is achieved, political access requires tremendous effort—especially on the part of rural schools of modest means, whose voice in state government is already marginalized in the money-talks sphere of political influence. In my experience, few superintendents regularly leave the district to lobby government officials—and for good reason. From my trips to Harrisburg during the Devon crisis, I knew that a visitation from a rural district to the legislative inner sanctum could be at times as welcome as a swarm of gnats, even though all discussions with politicians were professional in nature. Sus-ceptible to the school privatization agenda of the DeVos, Koch, and Heritage Foundations, even Senator Eichelberger was largely unsympathetic to the plight of the public schools in his district when it came to Governor Corbett's historic cuts to public education, which conservatives state-wide cleverly re-spun in the press as the largest state contribution to basic education in state history. It was an impressive hall of fiscal distortions that the Corbett administration had constructed—counting historically high PSERS contributions as part of the basic education subsidy, withdrawing state reimbursement for cyber school tuition, allowing cyber tuition levels to go unchecked with minimal accountability for results. Some might call this a Machiavellian compartmentalization of morality from politics. To me it was just part of the game. Still, the game reignited the fire in my belly. I had pestered the capital before—and even though I knew my years to retirement were numbered, I also knew that we must play the part of political gnats once again—this time for the benefit of public education statewide. To those closest to me, we called this our biggest fight.

Part of the effort involved educating legislators about the shortcomings of non-traditional schools. While some of them surely knew of the shortcomings, they did not want to hear about them, as the leaders of these schools were primary campaign contributors. On one occasion, after extensive letter writing and lobbying trips to Harrisburg to fight Senate Bill 1, which would divert public school funding to nontraditional schools at the brink of the fiscal cliff, Denny Murray and I along with other Blair County superintendents, (Paul Gallagher, Brian Toth, Linda Smith, Royce Boyd, and Rodney Green) orchestrated a meeting of state legislators with area school administrators, board members and teachers at Tyrone's high school cafeteria. Hundreds were in attendance to hear Representatives Mike Fleck and Jerry Stern and other representatives of the four IUs support the public school students' interests and to hear the Senate's Education Committee Chairman Jeffrey Picolla and John Eichelberger assail them. There was frank discussion on both sides, and while I presume few if any minds were changed, the real message of the meeting was this: we realize that the Republican-controlled Senate may have the votes to win the battle, but information campaigns like this will ensure that along with the Democratic-led House, our Republican allies, and state organizations, our successful public schools will win the war. We agreed as a group of Blair County superintendents that it was useless to meet with Senator Eichelberger, who had an unswervingly negative attitude toward public education in general.

Eventually, that is what happened. Public opinion swirled to rout the voucher bill—an end made possible by the groundswell of opinion generated by efforts like ours. Staff members from both Tyrone and Bellwood-Antis joined in the effort to expose the governor's unconstitutional agenda. One of our English staffers exploited the local media by drafting a three-part anti-voucher series, likening the governor's sales tactics to those exploited by infomercial gurus:

School Vouchers? Think Sham-Wow . . .

"It's like a chamois! It's like a towel! It holds up to 20 times its weight! It does all the work!" So says Vince, the slick-talking marketer who claims his wonder-rag will revolutionize the world of spills. Who wouldn't believe Vince? After testing its absorbency, *Consumer Reports* declared the truth: "It's like a rag. It absorbs about as much water as a sponge, a product with a long history of getting the job done at a reasonable cost."

Recently, Governor Corbett announced a possible 20% slashing of public school funds, and on top of this he has promised a Sham Wow alternative to your neighborhood school—a product that he and many legislators see as a cure to all that ails—a Voucher System.

As it stood, it meant little to the governor that the vast majority of Pennsylvanians, 65% according to a 2011 Omnibus Poll, did not want their tax dollars to be diverted from their neighborhoods into failing cyber schools, upscale private schools, or religious institutions—some of which might be hundreds of miles away from the original taxing jurisdiction. It is worth noting that at the time of that poll, the United States military rejected 9 out of every 10 cyber school students, citing as rationale what many parents already suspected—that cyber students too frequently lacked the ability to function in the highly disciplined social structure of the armed forces. The military has since changed its policy in this regard, probably under political pressure. While many parents choose cyber schools for all the right reasons, too many opt out of public education because the kids lack the coping skills or discipline to function in any institution; more than a few Tyrone parents opt out just to avoid truancy fines.

Policy-wise, the governor was largely tone-deaf to the statistical outcry that few cyber and charter schools were meeting the most basic academic expectations set forth by No Child Left

Behind. In the last year of NCLB in 2013, not a single cyber school had made AYP. Even Senator John Eichelberger neglected to acknowledge publically the bargain that Tyrone residents enjoyed through their public schools—namely, that Tyroners paid the 9th lowest property tax millage among the state's 500 school districts and yet enjoyed the highest achievement and growth scores in the state by a number of measures, returning to taxpayers a lot of bang for their buck. In at least one blog, Senator Eichelberger upbraided local teachers for contacting him through publically-financed equipment:

> I got some very interesting calls and emails today from public school folks. It is worth noting that many of the calls and emails came from school employees while on taxpayers' time and using taxpayer funded equipment. Certainly, any citizen has the right to address their elected officials, but using public resources to advance their personal agenda is inappropriate, unethical and perhaps illegal.

Eichelberger's point was well-taken in a business sense, but some outside the public school system did not find it honest or helpful. For example, Penn State Professor Timothy Slekar wrote in a rebuttal letter to the *Altoona Mirror*:

> On Eichelberger's blog posts, the senator found it offensive that public school employees would take time during their breaks or lunch or on their way to work to contact his office. According to the senator, if you're working for the state, you have no right to address your government. Interesting.

Slekar attacked the senator's claim that calls from teachers during the school day or from a district phone were unethical or illegal. He reasoned, "The state hired these teachers to advocate and do right by their students. It would seem to me that advocating for children during the hours of school is perfectly legal, maybe even mandatory." Slekar pointed to what he perceived to be Eichelberger's moral hypocrisy in sponsoring an unconstitutional bill:

> What about the senator? What was he doing during work hours at the expense of the taxpayers' using

taxpayer facilities? He was advocating breaking the law by passing an unconstitutional bill that would take resources from children, teachers and our local public schools. It seems a little unethical and slightly hypocritical?

In the months leading up to the vote on the historic Senate Bill 1 regarding the vouchers, when it became clear that the bill would garner the votes to pass, teachers like Bellwood-Antis' Tim Andrekovich cited what he saw as the senator's abandonment of local schools and urged him to do what the mounting ground-swell against the bill in the House had long ago proposed: stop enabling the relatively tax-free exploitation of the state's richest natural resource in the Marcellus Shale gas deposits. Instead, the state could use those tax revenues to help restore over-all public school funding to pre-fiscal cliff levels. Andrekovich did not mince words in rebuking Eichelberger's tone with questions that had answers that the senator wisely would not acknowledge:

April 5, 2011
Senator Eichelberger,
I would appreciate if you or someone on your staff could provide me the answers to the following questions at your earliest convenience. I apologize in advanced for the number of questions.
1. Can you please share with me the PSSA, PVAAS and AYP scores for the private and parochial schools within Blair County? Since you support creating competition, I would like to be able to accurately compare the job that our public, private and parochial schools are doing.
2. Since funding to public education has been cut by about 20% and funding for our state supported universities has been cut by about 50%, can the taxpayers of Pennsylvania expect the Governor and the Legislature to cut their budgets by about the same amounts?
3. Along those lines, teachers, professors, other university employees, and state workers are expected to take a pay freeze for this year. Since you claim to be a fiscal conservative, can the taxpayers of Pennsylvania count on you and all of the members of your staff to take a pay freeze too? Technically, you are a state employee and

we all should share the pain in these tough economic times . . .

4. Do you support taxing the Marcellus Shale natural gas drilling companies?

5. Would you be willing to introduce legislation that would cut the size of our state legislature in half? There are 435 members in the House of Representatives in Washington D.C. for over 310 million Americans but we have 253 members in the Pennsylvania Congress for a population of 12.7 million. That seems a bit excessive. Tens of millions of dollars would easily be saved by doing this.

One final thought, I find it disturbing that in your March 31st blog you stated, "I got my usual anti-freedom emails from public school employees." So anyone who disagrees with you or has a difference of opinion is to be considered anti-freedom? I always thought that in a democratic society, an open dialogue and discussion with ones elected represen-tative was valued. I am sure that those anti-freedom public school employees will use their constitutional rights during the next election.

I look forward to your response.

Sincerely,
Tim Andrekovich

John Eichelberger is a seasoned politician and a great public relations man. About the state-leading growth scores of schools in his own legislative district, Senator Eichelberger likely knew the truth. It simply would have not been politically advantageous for him to admit it. Consider his blog the day before the full Senate vote on Senate Bill 1. Not only were his statistical sources unsub-stantiated; they were either distorted or fictitious—and thus they effectively advanced his "failing schools" narrative:

Much of what I heard from public school employees today was about how well the current system works. It is important for people to understand that statewide our students come in 42nd out of the 50 states in SAT scores, we are in the bottom third in PSSA testing (perhaps as low as 45th), . . . and the majority of schools continued to raise taxes on the property owners back home.

The senator did not point out that in the nation's top-ranked states, fewer than 5% of American students even take the SAT (Scholastic Aptitude Test), a trend that statistically highlights the successes of the best and brightest kids and camouflages the shortcomings of the bottom 95%. Only three states ranking ahead of Pennsylvania in 2012 had a greater participation percentage [over 74%]. The state with the highest participation rate (Delaware at 100%) was ranked 50th' as any statistician would predict given such a fickle and politically-utilitarian predictor of school quality. It is little wonder that conservative critics rarely point to Delaware [a coveted tax haven for hundreds of millions of Pennsylvania corporate profits] as a poster-child of public school failure. Delaware's SAT rank—dead last in the nation with the nation's highest participation rate—is a poor reflection on the merit of its schools.

For a true national measure of his state's education quality, Eichelberger could have chosen the NAEP (National Assessment of Educational Progress, commonly called "the nation's report card"), which assesses a statistically reliable cross-section of students of all abilities—and on which his home state had demonstrated unparalleled growth over the previous eight years of increased and well-targeted funding. He could have done as Tim Andrekokich suggested and cited Blair County PVAAS scores, which in Tyrone's case were first in the state—with Altoona's also in the top 10%. Instead, he made the unsubstantiated claim about PSSA scores being "as low as 45th"—revealing a misconception that PSSA scores are nationally ranked or normed in some manner, which they are not. His parting salvo was a shot at burdensome property taxes, which in his own legislative district were among the lowest in the commonwealth. The Altoona Area School District at one point had gone close to two full decades without a single tax increase.

Also to his credit, the senator eventually responded to Andrekovich, albeit dismissively:

Mr. Andrekovich,
Obviously, you are connected to a public school and don't want to discuss, in a rational manner, the problems concerning the funding and performance of public schools. You know the answers to many of the questions you asked and won't accept my

answers on others I could answer. Instead of trying to take deflect your system's shortcomings onto the legislature, gas drilling or corporate America, I would suggest that you work to make public education better. You evidently feel that public education is perfect or, maybe, it isn't perfect, but can only be looked at when every other problem in Pennsylvania is fixed first. I don't share your view. I represent the interests of taxpayers and children.

You should as well.
John Eichelberger

Many school personnel believed the senator's idea of representing children and taxpayers interests in his legislative district was ultimately to help eradicate public education. I am more inclined to believe that John truly saw the value in Tyrone schools (or in any other school that he represented in his district). Perhaps, though, he believed that acknowledging this value was tantamount to endorsing public education across the state, which he did not wish to do. Clearly, his real political pushes were to tackle the educational dysfunction in the urban schools, where alternatives were limited, and to allow parochial and private schools there and around Tyrone to flourish, while fostering competition that would improve all schools. I agree with him on that point—Blair County schools and many of their teachers were fiercely competitive. The problem, though, was that the playing fields for public and private schools were not equal by any stretch, and that Senate Bill 1 would only exacerbate the disparity. He also knew that the fiscal cliff that we confronted was the most convenient juncture in state history to tip the scales in favor of private and cyber education.

At a time when Pennsylvania faced a $4 billion budget deficit, Corbett's proposals and Senate Bill 1 would create a new tax-funded program for private, parochial, and non-traditional school tuition, far from free.

Sending one child to a cyber-school already bled local taxpayers by as much as $16,000. Tyrone Area schools already sent over a half-million dollars a year out of town to cyber schools. Statewide, the expanded voucher system would cost taxpayers approximately $100 million in new state spending in the first year, and costs would increase rapidly. According to the Pennsylvanians Opposed to Vouchers Coalition, if less than one-third of eligible students received vouchers in each of the first three years under Senate Bill 1, the cost to taxpayers would rise to over $250 million in the second year. The cost would rise to more than a billion dollars by the third year as the program expanded to give vouchers to children currently enrolled in private and religious schools.

But the cybers and charters were far from scrupulous with the funding they received from taxpayers. While some cyber executives took advantage of skyboxes at professional sporting events, many did not take advantage of the non-union nature of their teaching forces to control salaries any better than did traditional public school administrators. Consider the 2008 salary of Abdus Salaam, an elementary teacher with 13 years of experience in the KIPP Academy Charter School, at $78,001. A teacher in the Tyrone Area School District with similar experience that year was paid $30,000 *less*—and yet contributed to superior student growth results.

From its pre-kindergarten program, ranked 3rd in the state, to its high school program ranked number one in PVAAS growth for two years in a row, Tyrone schools delivered superior quality for a modest price. But because of the lack of reassessment in the county, many residents were and are paying a disproportionate share of local property tax. School property taxes on a typical $100,000 market value home near the Gray Vets football field in the heart of town were $250-$450 a year. Conversely, a property on Engleman Drive near the high school yielded $1800 in school tax revenue, since no reassessment had been done since 1958. Now in 2014, the Blair County Commissioners have summoned the political courage to propose a reassessment that recognizes this longstanding need to equalize property tax values, as should have been done decades ago. With the projected reassessment of properties, reportedly a third of Tyrone residents will pay more, a third will pay less, and a third will remain at current levels. Quite literally, what many borough residents have paid for public education has been a fraction of their cable bills. In many urban and suburban districts statewide, by contrast, property tax rates often exceeded $5,000, with less comparable results at the other end.

While these numbers suggested that our county provided our kids an educational bargain, legislators state-wide feigned a different perspective. Their contention was that Senate Bill 1 would spur schools to compete, as if to imply that they had been shamefully slacking for the last decade or two. In reality, our local schools had been out-competing cyber schools for years—and while less wealthy rural districts like ours continued to out-perform the cybers on every measure of excellence, our budgets hemorrhaged with each student lost to inferior cybers that allowed kids to sidestep the high standards of our neighborhood schools. All that the voucher bill would spur would be swifter hemorrhaging of dollars away from our kids' classroom into those that failed to make AYP (Adequate Yearly Progress). Public schools like Tyrone's would still have the same fixed costs after the spread of vouchers, increasing pressure for local property tax increases. Buses would still need to drive the same routes, buildings would still need to be heated, floors would still need to be swept—these were hard brick-and-mortar realities.

Supporters had no trouble gleaning hard evidence that traditional schools outperformed cyber, charter, or parochial schools for that matter. All public schools were held to the same academic standards by No Child Left behind. But most charters and cyber schools failed to meet these standards. Few parochial schools had a clear idea how they were performing relative to their traditional public counterparts since they had no accountability for performance under the state's mandatory testing system. As for brick-and-mortar charter schools, the best ones in the nation were operated by KIPP, which was featured on *60-Minutes* during the fiscal crisis, on the cover of *Time*, and in the movie *Waiting for Superman*—a highly politicized documentary chronicling the trials and tribulations of poor urban students withering on waiting lists to super-human KIPP charter schools but unable to gain entry for lack of sufficient *spots* [translation, "*diverted public school funding*"]. While KIPP was certainly doing wonderful things in the city, Tyrone's neighborhood middle school had outscored KIPP on the PSSA the year that *Waiting for Superman* hit the box office. Our school had generated significantly greater growth overall per student in math and reading than had KIPP.

How low was low for the performance of charter and cyber schools? Consider that the average cyber school in the state had only 5.9% of their students score as advanced on the PSSA Writing test the year *Waiting for Superman* became the media lens for evaluating public education. The average brick-and-mortar charter school scored only 6.2% advanced, yet the state public school average was twice as great as this. PA Cyber, whose largesse had enabled it to sponsor the morning news ticker on WTAJ and to flood radio and television markets with Madison-Avenue-quality advertising spots, scored only 8.3% advanced. It deserved higher marks for marketing itself. Meanwhile, students at traditional neighborhood school Tyrone High scored 81.6%

advanced among all students tested. State politicians should have raised a few eyebrows at ads in the local papers luring children to nearby Tuscarora Blended Cyber. Those ads made no mention of its advanced-level writing scores—a dismal 2.6%. As the following chart reveals, although only 7% of the state's 541 school districts were charters or cyber-charters, their high schools comprised 40% of the bottom ten in terms of value-added (value-lost?) growth:

State Rank	2011 11th Grade PSSA Results for Reading, Writing, Math, and Science	Value Added
541	West Side CTC	-395
540	Lawrence County CTC	-390
539	Perseus House Charter School	-290
538	Solanco School District	-285
537	Academy Charter School	-277
536	Shenandoah Valley School District	-262
535	PA Learners Online Regional Cyber	-256
534	Weatherly Area School District	-251
533	Susq-Cyber Charter School	-248
532	Columbia Borough School District	-239

Source: https://pvaas.com. November 25, 2011.

More recently, the state has transitioned to rating schools on a more sweeping measure, the Pennsylvania School Performance Profile [SPP], which considers all testing [SAT, PSAT, PSSA, Keystone, and NOCTI (National Occupational Competency Testing Institution)] at all grade levels—as well as attendance and graduation rates—and awards points for both proficiency and growth. The SPP results are equally telling, with 70.0 points on a 100.00-point scale the mark of a school that is succeeding to some degree. While Tyrone schools continue to rank at the top of their intermediate unit (with an 88.8 mark at the high school, for example), the state's cyber schools continue to languish—not one of them is making the 70.0 mark of "beginning success" established by PDE. Still the cybers continue to siphon away hundreds of thousands of dollars from Tyrone area taxpayers, many of whom continue to send their children to cyber schools— despite all the numerical evidence exposing their ineffectiveness:

Cyber School SPP Ratings: 2014

21st Century Cyber CS	66.0
Achievement House CS	37.5
ACT Academy Cyber CS	28.9
Agora Cyber CS	42.4
ASPIRA Bilingual Cyber Charter School	39.0
Central PA Digital Lrng Foundation CS	48.8
Commonwealth Connections Academy CS	52.2
Education Plus Academy Cyber CS	50.0
Esperanza Cyber CS	47.7
Pennsylvania Cyber CS	55.5
Pennsylvania Distance Learning CS	50.9
Pennsylvania Leadership CS	59.3
Pennsylvania Virtual CS	63.4

Source: http://www.paschoolperformance.org. November 11, 2014.

Along the same line, fresh scholarly research of the largest student comparison group ever studied exposed the elemental misconception of anti-public school / pro-gas industry supporters. When academic achievement comparisons were adjusted to account for student characteristics such as race and disability status, public school students nationwide performed better than private school students. Researchers at the University of Illinois recently analyzed the test scores of more than 340,000 4th and 8th grade students in 13,000 traditional public schools, charter schools, and private schools on the NAEP commonly called "the nation's report card." They found that "demographic differences between students in public and private schools more than account for the relatively high raw scores of private schools . . . after controlling for these differences, the presumably advantageous 'private school effect' disappeared, and even reversed in most cases." In his official evaluation of the Milwaukee voucher program, Professor John Witte of the University of Wisconsin at Milwaukee found that "achievement (of voucher students), as measured by standardized tests, was no different than the achievement of Milwaukee Public School students." Cleveland's voucher program was evaluated with similar results.

The most deleterious aspect of the voucher bill was that poorer districts like Tyrone's would suffer losses much more severe than would wealthier districts. I am not certain that many legislators fully considered this feature of the bill. One of our public relations pieces in *The Daily Herald* simplified the complicated financial inequity in culinary terms:

> Picture your school district budget as a banana split. Over 66% of the budget covers the scoops of ice cream—that's the huge chunk that comes from the state. Another 6% is the slice of banana underneath—that comes from the federal government. What comes from our local property taxes, the remaining 28%, is barely enough to cover the whipped cream, a few chopped nuts, and a cherry if we're lucky.
>
> What we must remember is that our state tax dollars [the big 66% chunk] will go to vouchers. That means that when Tyrone students leave the district, they take the ice cream with them and leave behind a banana slice and a few peanuts. At $8000 per regular education child, it cost our schools a quarter-million dollars to send 30 students away with vouchers. What about State College students? Since State College receives only 10% of its funding from the state, a student there leaving with a voucher takes only a few peanuts and leaves behind a mother-load of ice cream plus the banana. Instead of losing $250,000 for 30 voucher kids, State College, already wealthy by comparison, loses relatively little.
>
> Poorer districts like ours will be the biggest losers under Senate Bill 1's Voucher System. As PARSS forewarns, "If ten eligible students from [a wealthy district like State College or] York Suburban elect to use their vouchers, that district will experience a loss of $19,620 in its state subsidy while, if ten eligible students from [a poorer district like Tyrone or] Purchase Line School District use their voucher, that district will experience a loss of $112,770."

Where was the equity for the poor rural districts of Blair County? At a meeting of legislators and school leaders at the

Tyrone Area High School in March of 2011, our senators had no answers. All they could say was that "the new competition will make all schools better." This might have been true of schools that were either persistently failing or not already hustling to win, like the many lagging schools in Harrisburg and Philadelphia—but not of ours in Blair County, where Tyrone, Bellwood, and Altoona all delivered top-of-the-state results. The bill's supporters acted like the playing field was level for public and non-traditional schools, yet their bill did not require the latter schools to report to parents how their students performed against local schools on state exams, a standard of quality from which they were exempt. Because teacher salaries exceeded $100,000 in a few districts in the state, it was easy for some senators to paint all of them with the same brush.

In truth, Tyrone teacher salaries were among the lowest in the state, in the mid-forties, right in line with the income of the average area plumber according to *Salary.com*—but with a master's degree and continuing education credits required by law until retirement. Tyrone parents and taxpayers expected schools to deliver on quality. They had done that. They expected schools to keep their taxes low. Although all taxes pose a burden, two of our Blair County's school systems [Tyrone and Altoona] had millage rates among the lowest ten in the state. They expected schools to be safe places that supported their values despite the increasingly valueless society that swarmed outside schoolyard doors. In turn, we expected teachers to motivate and rehabilitate the abused, disruptive, and violent students that society handed them. And all of this many Blair County public schools did, although there was not a parochial, charter, or cyber school in the state that was required by state law to do the same. We were also sure that under the governor's voucher system, as had already happened in voucher systems nationally; many special needs students would either be rejected by or kicked out of voucher-receiving schools. Over time, troubled kids would accumulate disproportionately in our neighborhood schools, as would many students whose special learning needs cut too deeply into the voucher-receiving school's operating margin. Gradually, as non-traditional schools cherry-picked the students they deemed most academically and athletically suitable, the financial and human resources that neighborhood schools needed to rehabilitate troubled students would be strained. Parochial, private, and charter schools might choose not to deal with this strain, simply kicking the fiscally unattractive student back into the public school system. The tilt in the playing field was clear to all the competitors.

In addition to all of these expectations of our public schools, parents also expected them to make memories for their kids, to become indelible parts of their character and experience. They wanted their kids to play in a marching band, to pledge a flag, to go to a prom, to argue a case in a mock trial court, to applaud a classmate, to snap a picture for a school newspaper, to get praise from a coach, to sign a yearbook, to cry on the shoulder of a counselor when she had no other shoulder to cry on, to have eye-contact with a teacher who cared whether the student understood. They expected challenges for their kids that would get them out of their pajamas in the morning and make them better students and better people. The cyber schools could not offer these neighborhood-school experiences. Nevertheless, Senate Bill 1 passed, but the victory would be short-lived.

The truth about unfair competition and the public's good regard for public education prevailed through a number of respected polls. Corbett's voice was not the voice of the vast majority of Pennsylvanians. Eventually, the reelection hopes of public education's most contentious nemesis began to wither, and his allies for the time abandoned his agenda to dismantle Pennsylvania public education.

That did not mean that local senators would be more inclined to show greater love for public education. Consider this post from Eichelberger's edition of *"John's Blog"* two years after the demise of SB 1:

School Property Taxes Have Increased Far Above the Rate of Inflation and Well Beyond the Increase of Both Sales and Income Taxes

Article posted on October 15, 2013

We're back in session. I spent most of the morning at a hearing on doing away with school property taxes. The Independent Fiscal Office (IFO) issued a report on SB 76 and HB 76, both bills deal with shifting school property taxes to sales and income. It was interesting to note that since 1993, school property taxes have increased far above the rate of inflation and well beyond the increase of both sales and income taxes. The report concluded that the funding under the new tax structure would fall short of property tax estimates over the next 5 years. What they didn't state is that by providing a more reasonable increase in funding, the schools would have to be careful with their spending and the taxpayers would be saddled with a smaller tax burden. I was asked just yesterday about this issue from a lady in Fulton County. I hear about excessive school property taxes often and hope that the legislature can get one of these bills or something similar across the finish line soon.

—John

John re-embraced his constituency—the politically wise move for him. I harbor him no ill will for it. Some might say he skirted the truth rather than reinvented it. I have rummaged through John's blog posts for the last two years for a single acknowledgement of Blair County's low school tax rates or its high academic growth rates, both of which are matters of public record and facts that a senator could boast of freely in Harrisburg. Especially in the run-up to the 2014 gubernatorial election, the legislative spotlight of the governor and the Republican House had shone strictly on the "Investment" half of ROI (Return on Investment) as a fresh bill to abolish property taxes. Strangely, this bill emerged at a time when Pennsylvania funded only 36% of the total cost of public education, ranking it near the bottom of the nation in state-support. All the while, minimal if any praise was extended during the campaign to public schools for their phenomenal "Return" on the state's comparatively paltry investment. PSBA Executive Director Nathan Mains pointed to the 2014 nation-leading ACT (American College Testing) results of Pennsylvania students as large-scale evidence of our schools' excellence: "Studies continue to point to educational achieve-ments in Pennsylvania. These nation-leading scores demonstrate to the entire country the academic ability of Pennsylvania students, the dedication of our teachers, and the world-class quality of our education system."

But public-school-friendly facts like these, with 2014 ACT scores "exceeding the national averages by at least ten percentage points," rarely make it to Harrisburg unless you take them there—or bring Harrisburg to you, as we did in the four IUs of Central Pennsylvania. Such facts shatter the opposition's central talking point: that public education is a colossal waste of taxpayer money and must be privatized—not to shelter billionaires like the Marcellus Shale gas drillers or the Koch brothers from taxes, of course, but to "save the kids." High quality and effective public education is a cornerstone of the American Dream and of our democracy's promise of opportunity for all. We must make it, too, prevail.

Principles of Prevailing

- ✓ Deceit is a part of politics, as is feigning ignorance and refusing to address the full truth.
- ✓ If you intend to influence them, you must show politicians due respect.
- ✓ Lawmakers for their own survival still focus on the voices that speak most loudly and those that can get closest to their ears. In legislative ears, money buys that access.
- ✓ The superintendent's challenge is to gain access to legislators through organizations, the press, letter writing, in-person meetings, or more creative channels.

10 | Negotiate Wisely

Einstein knew people as well as he knew astrophysics. A superintendent must take Einstein's advice to heart and treat everyone with respect, even when a person has personally betrayed and deceived him. The pages of this book are filled with such betrayals. Political alliances and personal deceptions make respectful treatment difficult—but not impossible.

Perhaps the most nettlesome region of superintendence in this regard is negotiating collective bargaining agreements. Respect between labor and management is a must in schools because, invariably, what happens at the bargaining table spills over into the classrooms and hallways after the ink is dry. In a world of infinite resources, compromise would not be necessary, but shredding core principles or fiscal solvency can compromise the ability of the institution to deliver on its mission. I do not believe in applying a strict business model to our schools, but any institution must attend to metrics of cost and quality. Minding those metrics while compensating staff in a principled manner is the bugaboo. Attending to these five principles ultimately guided us through the nettles, especially in two very memorable negotiations—one in 1972, the other decades later in 2007:

1. Remember who you work for: the school board, the taxpayers, and the kids.
2. Be firm on principled issues.
3. Be patient. [Allow public opinion time to validate your position, as it did in 1972-73]
4. Pay attention to the comparables to make sure the marketplace is not creating a flight of quality.
5. Find ways to offer differential pay to teachers.

During my first year as superintendent, union negotiations were particularly thorny. The state's landmark Public Employee Act 195[11] had been signed into law two years earlier in 1970; it was not long before Pennsylvania ranked first in the nation in teacher strikes. Tyrone teachers voted formally to organize as a union for the first time in their history in May of 1970, and a year later they became the Tyrone Area Education Association (TAEA) with 71 votes in favor. As it turned out, 47 teachers voted in favor of a rival union—the Tyrone Independent Teacher Association— and 2 teachers voted against any union representation. Another 17 did not vote at all. Obviously, there were clear differences of opinion within their ranks, as is common. Nonetheless, heady with newfound bargaining rights that the union leadership was eager to exercise, we began to talk.

It was not long before contract negotiations had the two parties at opposite ends. With collective bargaining in such an embryonic stage, management and employees operated on a divisive "We" versus "They" basis, unlike the talks of the new millennium, when staff and administration worked together to find common ground and agree on what was best for all stakeholders. A teacher named Mr. Wunder, President of the Tyrone Area Education Association, pushed early for complete medical coverage for teachers and their families. The board was making a very strong stance that we would cover the employees only. Other issues were of concern, of course, but he did not waste time taking the union's concerns directly to the press—a move that we

---

11 This granted teachers and other public employees the right to strike. Act 195 continues to define the framework of public-sector collective bargaining in Pennsylvania. Source http://ballotpedia.org/Pennsylvania_Act_195_(1970)

try to avoid today in order to engender good faith bargaining and to reduce public pressure on either party. Not all districts adopt this stance, but negotiations can be intellectually and emotionally complicated endeavors that require fact-checking, changes of stance, and changes of heart. Additionally, it is a courtesy and a sign of respect to agree to terms without the public as a third party directing the agenda. If either party overreaches, the public will ultimately let them know when the details become public—one of the many virtues of having a small-town newspaper. Mr. Wunder fully expected to tap that resource, but he did not fully anticipate how it might tap back.

At a scheduled in-service meeting on August 29, 1972, Mr. Wunder made a very unusual request. He told us to give him about fifteen minutes to present our latest stance to the faculty so that we could get a vote and thus be able to move ahead. We gave him the fifteen minutes that he requested. At this time Administrative Assistant Mr. Barrett and I were walking back to the cafeteria where the faculty had held their meeting, and as we approached the cafeteria doors, the staff rolled out of the building in droves. Mr. Barrett and I asked what was going on, and they exclaimed they were going on strike—without any opportunity to talk matters through and compromise. It was a lesson learned: Mr. Wunder had led us down a bad path. It's difficult to express the rage I felt at his betrayal—but I worked actively to let it go. The vote to strike was 72 to 38; the strike lasted only three days, but so much happened in those days that it seemed like weeks.

As we later discovered, Wunder published a series of prepared rationales for the strike months before he had formally declared one. In a weekly feature in the *Tyrone Daily Herald* titled "Tyrone Teachers Talk," Wunder's first installment was called "What Triggered the School Strikes?" To stir up public sympathy and anxiety, the title brazenly referenced the rash of school strikes that had erupted statewide since the passage of Public Employee Act 195. Five full months prior to declaring a strike, Wunder underscores two key points in the article: that a strike will affect everyone adversely and that the union will be looking closely at Blair County comparables:

> Nobody gains when negotiations break down and work stoppages result. When this happens in a school district, the buildings must be heated and maintained; yet no students are there. Parents like to have children finish school terms on time so the family is free to take a vacation. Children do better

during the cooler months of the year when the rooms are more comfortable.

It must be remembered that the government-run schools are the property of all the people, and their interest must prevail. We must also realize that no community can live as an island unto itself. If the Altoona teachers are provided with certain conditions, it won't be long before the adjacent school districts will be providing like conditions. Good labor relations is [sic] the mark of sound management and will net the community a high quality staff; . . . poor relations work just the opposite, and the entire educational system tends to fall apart.

In subsequent installments, while negotiations were still in progress, Wunder insisted in making talks a public affair in his weekly newspaper feature. He wasted no time in publishing salary and benefit data released by the fact-finder's report of September 7, 1971 indicating that Tyrone salaries were $255 and $483 below the average state minimum and maximum respectively—a gap that equated to roughly 3.7%. In historical terms, Blair County salaries though the decades of my tenure regularly lagged the state averages, often by as much as 10%. So as dismal as the $6,900 may seem today as the starting bachelor of science salary figure for a Tyrone teacher in 1972, today's Tyrone starting bachelor of science salary of $41,280 is in roughly the same position relative to the state average, slightly below it, with Tyrone's maximum bachelor of science salary now $69,303 also below state average. Wunder also emphasized that the district had decreased the percentage of money spent on teacher salaries by 10% from 1968 to 1971, an amount equal to $1,630 per teacher. He made no mention of the decreasing enrollment that necessitated the staff cut-backs accounting for that 10% reduction—he left it open to interpretation by the *Herald* readership that salaries had been cut by 10%, which of course had not happened.

These propaganda pieces trundled into April, with Wunder expanding the comparables from neighboring teacher unions to the state trooper union, soliciting the public to consider the indispensable role of the teaching profession. After all, aside from a man in handcuffs, rare was the complaint about a state cop's pay:

One thing more to consider, in 1968 a board of arbitration awarded the state policemen of Pennsylvania an 11½ percent cost-of-living increase. This made the starting salary for newly appointed troopers $9,258.96 with a high school diploma. The starting salary in the Tyrone School District in 1968 was $6300.00 for a newly-appointed teacher . . . We think the police deserve the salary they are paid for they have an important task in our society. But answer this—what would our society be like today without good teachers to guide the young?

If Wunder erred at all in these public tracts, he did so in talking of fiscal concerns so early in the game. The public received the initial and long-lasting impression one would expect from any negotiations—that the real issues were monetary. So by the time Wunder wrote his May 3, 1972 tract, the public already understood clearly what the newly formed union cared about most— money. Understanding his misfire, Wunder tried to change direction:

Act 195 states that anything may be considered a negotiable item as long as it does not fall under the domain of "inherent managerial policy." This is where the crux of all the negotiating problems arise . . . The teachers believe that class size is a negotiable item; the school board does not. The teachers believe that preparation time is a negotiable item—the school board does not . . . Most teachers in the Tyrone School District would have sacrificed their $200 raise last year if they could have had a reduction in class size or perhaps adequate preparation time. These improvements would certainly not result in money in the teachers' pockets but these are the things that are high on the priority list.

This would be one of Wunder's last journalistic expeditions to net public favor. Had he emphasized the class-size angle earlier, showing concern over compromised learning and crowded rooms, he might have caught more fish. Instead, he became rapt in the injustice of lagging comparables, forgetting all the while that administrator salaries also lagged state averages by similar margins—and for good reason: Tyrone household income also lagged Pennsylvania's household income. While teachers in most communities should expect to be paid more than the average resident because of their more advanced education and training, they cannot expect blue-collar residents who work year-round and make less than teachers to express much empathy unless the disparities are extreme. Still, Wunder had seized the opportunity to shift to issues pertaining to "the improvement of the educational system" as the *Herald* reported just weeks before the strike. The union opined that class sizes were enormous—as high as 48 students filling a math room according to Wunder's count in an August 26 interview—and that the Board refused to address the issue in talks, claiming that it was management's right to determine how full is too full. Other teachers tried to run interference for Wunder, like Linda Strong, a third-grade instructor who penned a letter to the editor of the *Herald* in which she quibbled about non-monetary issues like the board's proposals "to lengthen the school day [by] 15 minutes" and to demand attendance at meetings "a minimum of four hours in length per month at the close of the school day." Again, carping about work hours gained minimal traction with a public that already worked 8-hour days opposed to our teachers' 7.25 hours, and year-round at that. Additionally, Wunder's hyperbolic statistics regarding class size were called into question by the 1971 findings of educational consultant Dr. Walter J. DeLacy, who conducted a site study of the district and determined that only one class in the district—one that "met sixth period on Wednesdays in room 205"—exceeded 40—and that figure was 42. The range in the high school was 24-38; the median was closer to 30 for the junior high, and the most common range for the grade school was 26-28. These numbers were not ideal, but Wunder's public overstatement of the truth did not garner him any favors.

Having sat by patiently for months while Wunder waged a one-sided media assault that weakened his own cause, we finally responded with a brief article explaining the complications of balancing a school budget. The upshot was that stagnant real estate values and drastically decreasing enrollment meant a much smaller revenue pie. Despite that decline, we pointed out that teaching staff numbers had actually increased at the junior and senior high school from 81.5 in 1968 to 85 in 1971 and that elementary teaching staff remained steady. These figures deflated Wunder's insinuation that we did not care about large class sizes. We had addressed the issue incrementally with additional staff hires—and would continue to do so as funding became available.

We fully recognized the link between class size and quality, but fixing the problem immediately would only cripple the district financially, making significant staff raises unlikely in the future.

So as we approached the strike date, these were the most germane issues and positions:

- **Length of work day.** Board: 7.5 hours; TAEA: rejection.
- **Attendance at Meetings.** Board: 4 hours; TAEA: rejection.
- **Insurance.** Board: Full employee coverage with up to $21.00/month for dependents. TAEA: Full coverage for the entire family.
- **Emergency Days.** Board: 2; TAEA: 2 plus 1 personal day.
- **Class Size and Preparation Periods.** Board: non-negotiable.
- **Salary.** Board: a two-year deal on $7,200 to $13,200 scale by 1973-74, with minimum $600 raises each year. TAEA: accepted.

Other issues littered the table, but these were of minimal import and had not been aired in the press as extensively if at all. It is well worth noting that salary was not a point of dispute at this juncture, days before the strike, making Wunder's looming betrayal all the more unexpected. In a last minute salvo, he responded in an interview that increased staff was needed, especially a nurse who would not have to travel to multiple school buildings to meet the urgent health concerns of students:

> Another item that the school board refuses to negotiate . . . is the need for extra specialists in the school district," he argued. "Presently there is one nurse serving the five elementary schools. We feel this is inadequate to say the least. Let me pose a hypothetical question. What would happen to your child if he were injured in a serious accident at [Jefferson] School while the nurse responsible for his safety and well-being was occupied at [Madison]? We think this situation bears immediate attention. What does your school district think? We don't know, they have refused to negotiate this item since it falls under "inherent managerial policy."

Mr. Wunder had a point here, one that we had already planned to address promptly. He made other valid points as well on the day before striking, especially related to teacher turn-over, a trend that we shared great concern over and which we also had attempted to mitigate through increased hiring amid dwindling revenues. These were not issues to which we were cold, but as this was the first collective contract negotiation in our history, we would not discuss managerial issues in this highly precedential context, as was our prerogative and philosophy. We were fully aware that we had lost 32 members of our teaching staff over the last decade from 1962 to 1972 to schools within a 35-mile radius of us—some of whom were great teachers, some of whom we had wished would leave. Their flight represented about three teachers per year, or roughly 2% of staff. This is not an extraordinary number for any organization, especially one whose revenues cannot support compensation above the norm. Decades later, in 2006-07, when six teachers left for Bellwood and Hollidaysburg en masse, we knew that we needed to negotiate the means to retain quality—and that we did. Many of these were outstanding professionals, and their departure was a barometer of decreasing staff quality that could not be reversed without bargaining. TAEA negotiator Vicky Aults indicated that the 2001 "catch-up" contract passed with a 99-8 vote. I concurred by applauding the teachers during the Devon crisis for "accepting a less competitive figure" and clarifying that the new contract's intent was "to keep good teachers in their employment and to be very competitive with surrounding districts in attracting new teachers." And that we did.

So through the years we stood firm on principles of management rights and of rewarding quality. Mr. Wunder was an outstanding individual with incredible professional merit, but collective bargaining had ushered in an age that forced us to pay all teachers the same regardless of merit. He was carrying the banner of that age and would soon shake it on a picket. A photograph in the *Herald* on August 30 showed five teachers along Clay Avenue in front of the high school carrying signs that read "We'd Rather Talk Than Walk" and "No Contract No Work,"— and the teachers were smiling lightheartedly. The reporter noted in the caption that they were "enjoying it." If they had any inkling how the public was perceiving their smiles, they would have wiped them into scowls. It was not only the first teacher strike in Tyrone history; it was the first in the history of Blair County since Act 195 took effect. More than 3,500 students were affected. They were not universally happy.

Some students fought back, another costly union miscalculation. On the second day of the strike, 34 students wrote to the *Herald* editor. They opposed the strike, indicating that the "end result will be antagonism between the teachers and the students. We are only looking out for our welfare." The students also mentioned the upcoming football game with Bellwood-Antis—the traditional Backyard Brawl as it has come to be known, the first game of every season. The PIAA ruled that week that the team would be restricted from practicing during an official strike. Coach Steve Magulick, a Tyrone teacher, expressed his regret. "At least the kids can get together on their own and work out in shorts," he lamented, "I'm hoping they take the initiative to do so."

The students did not stop at editorializing. They manned picket lines of their own. Children at the Friendship School brandished signs that read "We Want To Go To School," "We're Suffering," "We're For Negotiating," as they swirled in a large circle around the playground grass. Meanwhile, high school student picketers brandished pickets that read "Start the Eagle Machine"—a call to the gridiron, perhaps—and "Compromise is Paradise"—a sideways nod to the 1970 Joni Mitchell social protest lyric "they paved paradise and put up a parking lot" still popular at the time. The students blamed the teachers for the strike. The *Altoona Mirror* indicated that the student protestors were angry because teachers were "using the football program as leverage to settle the strike and get their demands." An *Altoona Mirror* article the following day was even more caustic, featuring a few youngsters sitting on the steps of the Madison Elementary School and chanting, "Teachers, teachers are no good; chop them up for kindling wood." An unnamed administrator passing by saw no humor in the display and lamented, "The sad thing of it all is the long, long friendships that can never be patched up."

If the student bodies of both schools pulled no punches in the press, the community was no less brutal. The sneering ranged from confused to malicious, as the following sampling of public opinion from the *Herald* indicated:

> I, myself, do not really understand what the teachers are striking for. Every time I hear them talk I hear a different issue being named as the reason for what they are doing.

> The utilization of demands and the threat of strikes has taken many of these young men and women out

from under the "Professional" category and put them under one labeled "Militant Unionist."

Congratulations, Teachers: you've closed our schools . . . You say your working conditions are bad. Try ours. I would love to have a job all daylight, 15 days off for Christmas, three or four for Thanksgiving and Easter and all Saturdays and Sundays off. And we are the people who pay your wages.

But the most lethal attack perhaps came from Wunder's own faculty, four of whom went on record protesting the union's actions. Donna Bashor, Marjorie Walker, Debra Nearhoof, and Vickie Aults (who later became a TAEA President) announced their intention to cross the picket lines and to report to work. "You don't help kids by keeping them out of school," they announced in the *Altoona Mirror*. Bashor in particular criticized the union leadership: "If the teachers are really concerned about the students and not about personal economics," she editorialized, "why all the talk about money? I see the real issue not to be one of providing what is best for the student, but one of power. Who is going to control this district? Will it be the school board, whom I feel should, or will the TAEA?" In a *Herald* piece, Bashor attacked the intimidation tactic that the union leadership employed to convince teachers to vote. Instead of a secret ballot, members were forced to stand to indicate their voice: "Is this why some teachers did not vote at all? . . . Wasn't this a vote of intimidation? How can teachers be respected by parents and taxpayers when they are led like sheep [by their union leaders], apathetic sheep who have little interest in protecting their own rights?"

With virtually every constituency against them, the teachers abandoned their strike after three days. The vote to approve the contract was unanimous, all 100 teachers agreeing to the exact salary, insurance, preparation time, and class size conditions that the board originally proposed. Donna Bashor was correct. This strike was very much about power, and that power rested with the school board and the public that the board represented. Teachers saved a little face with our consent to "meet and discuss" issues of managerial policy, and we did agree to hire another itinerant nurse to meet student needs more responsively. We extended the school day by 15 minutes, but we limited after school meetings to three, as the union requested.

As a superintendent, one often witnesses a huge gulf between reality and perception. One of the most common misperceptions that folks have shared with me over the decades is that I wielded Geppetto-like command over school boards, that especially in negotiations, I tugged the strings and that both the agenda and the board were my puppets. Understanding my interest and aptitude in school finance, a lot of folks cannot imagine any other dynamic. When I declared prior to negotiation sessions that I would be in the background for consultation purposes only, that the board was in control, I regularly fielded looks of incredulity from union members. The reality was that I never overstepped my consultant role in all the contracts that I observed. Board members—who on many occasions were more parsimonious with taxpayer money than I was —directed talks and approved proposals.

I still recall a contract meeting that was at a standstill over a $5 a year difference in salary. All other issues had been settled, with the parties this close to a pact. I said to the board member, a local farmer whom I deeply respect, "Come on now, we're talking about a six-pack of beer here. If you'll settle this, I'll buy you one." The board member smiled and conceded on the spot, and every-one smiled. This anecdote reflects the way I exerted influence, with gentle cajoling and occasional insight from stage-right, but never barking orders from a director's chair. What many union negotiators failed to recognize was how often I openly negotiated for their cause with the board. This would have shocked them, for sure, particularly Mr.Wunder, who would later understand my meaning. One board that I recall entering talks with had the perception that a 0% raise was possible. They held to that line for quite some time until they were convinced otherwise. Right or wrong, there have been few if any comparables for multi-year salary freezes in public education. Those ignoring that reality might as well order picket signs for their local union.

Through the entire 1972 strike ordeal, I was true to my five principles. I remembered for whom I worked, the board and the kids, even though I fully understood the teachers' plight. I was firm and patient on the issues that mattered most—and those were not necessarily all fiscal ones. Remember that the teacher strike was a power-play, not necessarily a money-grab. It was a pissing contest with a newly-formed union trying to mark its territory and going about it in all the wrong ways. So we were firm on issues of managerial priority, unlike many districts that had conceded to such demands with ludicrous consequences: 100-plus page contracts with labyrinthine clauses and stipulations riddled with inefficiencies and cost-drivers. By contrast, ours was a Spartan document; we committed to lean language that promised we would do "everything administratively possible" to provide a period of preparation time, and we reduced class sizes to levels that today foster state-leading academic growth. We had the patience to give the union all the rope it needed to hang itself, to allow public opinion time to validate the board's positions on power and control. We attended to the comparables, and we addressed them gradually over a number of contracts so that the district could remain on sound fiscal ground.

By 2007, our teachers received raises in excess of 7%, and we peeled back insurance premium shares from 5% to a goose egg, the first time that such an insurance concession had ever been granted in state history, according to PSEA representative Sid Young. We realized that high-quality teachers were fleeing at an unhealthy rate and that such measures could stem the tide. Within five years our faculty passed nearly 50 bargaining units in average salary, and the value of their salary scale now equals the Blair County average. But their union leaders approached their negotiations in the proper way—organized with facts, not veiled threats; discreetly, not publically; with clear emphasis on the impact on student learning, not just on their paychecks; with sensitivity rather than callousness to the politics that the Board had to confront. With such a union, it was easy to devise ways outside of a collective bargaining agreement to reward excellent teaching—to find ways both to pay and "pay respect" to teachers differentially. We initiated with the help of an anonymous donor a Distinguished Educator award—three per year—to offer $1,000 in tax-free money to teachers whose students spoke highly of them during exit interviews prior to graduation. We funded attractive stipends for extra responsibility duties to coach faculty members, to serve as deans of students, and to assume special education roles. It took decades to resurrect the "Us" relationship from the "We/They" ruins of the 1970s strike, but contract negotiations can be opportunities for such resurrections to happen. Forgiveness and respect are as probable as you choose to make them, and when they seem most improbable, I recall the words of Desmond Tutu: "Without forgiveness, there is no future."

Years later, Dr.Wunder became a principal and later a superintendent at Clearfield Area School District. While I was still superintendent at Tyrone, he indirectly apologized to me for his actions in 1972, hijacking a scheduled in-service meeting to foment a strike. He acknowledged that he did what he had to do, and I nodded to recognize that there were no hard feelings. I saw him at his grandson's graduation recently. He shared with me that he is suffering from chronic illness, and my heart grew heavy. We remain good friends—a fertile relationship where there was once scant ground for respect.

He was always in my prayers.

Principles of Prevailing

- ✓ Respect everyone at the negotiating table, but remember who you work for—the board and the kids.
- ✓ What happens at the bargaining table—both good and bad—spills over into the classroom.
- ✓ Shredding core principles or fiscal solvency can compromise the ability of a school district to deliver on its mission.
- ✓ Compensate staff in a principled manner. Pay attention to the comparables—do not sacrifice quality staff. Remember that a teacher strike is sometimes a power-play, not necessarily a money-grab.
- ✓ Stand firm on principles of management rights and of rewarding quality.
- ✓ Allow board members to direct talks and approve proposals. Serve only as a consultant.
- ✓ Expect deception—but do not rush to call it out.

"Gilded tombs do worms enfold."
—William Shakespeare
The Merchant of Venice, Act 2.7.

"My fellow citizens: To a few of us today, this is a solemn and most momentous occasion; and yet, in the history of our Nation, it is a commonplace occurrence. The orderly transfer of authority . . . routinely takes place as it has for almost two centuries and few of us stop to think how unique we really are. In the eyes of many in the world, [what] we accept as normal is nothing less than a miracle."
—Ronald Reagan

11 | Massage the Transition of Authority

T he scale may be smaller, but the consequences are proportionately weighty. Whether on the international stage of a United States president or on the local stage of a public school superintendent, attention must be paid to the politics of transition. Decades of successful policies, practices, and results can vaporize under the heat of a new administration's ardor. Sometimes the call for change under new administration is both legitimate and necessary. At other times the call is for change's sake only—a superficial desire to look progressive and proactive without regard to substance. This occurring in an era when the average longevity of a superintendent in Pennsylvania is three years, according to the Pennsylvania School Boards Association. This brand of change is particularly pernicious in a small district, initiated not for the benefit of kids as much as for the benefit of a résumé-building candidate eager to hop on to a more lucrative gig in suburbia. Perhaps the worst call for change is the one attached to a long-suppressed ideological agenda or vendetta. These changes, too, are often undertaken without consultation, consensus, or research and are not so much proactive as reactive endeavors—in particular reactions against the trends, policies, and staff members that bolstered the appeal and efficacy of the previous administration. Our immersion in such ideological power struggles over the years prompted us to exercise due diligence in seeking a successor. Fortunately, we had on our administrative team a potential successor who had proven her mettle through many of the power struggles that we had endured.

One of many letters of recommendation written in support of Cathy Harlow referenced these transition-massaging considerations:

A Recommendation for Ms. Cathy Harlow
November 20, 2012

In the search for a district superintendent, a lot of statistics compete for attention. One of the most vital may be this one: turnover rate. In New Jersey public schools, one out of every three school CEO's leaves the job each year. In Pennsylvania, school leaders last four or five years on average, often leaving behind fragmented programs and distressed finances. Rarely do these fly-by-night school leaders experience the execution of a long-term vision or cull the wisdom that comes from sustained mentorship. This is a sobering thought—one that underscores a flaw in the standardized selection practices employed by too many Pennsylvania schools. In an attempt to embrace new "blood" or expand options, districts too often write off internal candidates who embody the very characteristics they seek. Dismissing hiring-from-within as limiting and parochial, committees court candidates who gush about passion for kids, who rehearse glib interview gambits, who brandish resumes listing schools "fortunate to secure their services" (for a few years each, of course), and who make bold promises they have no idea how to keep. Before long, such candidates scoop up their severance packages and

exit through a corridor of broken trust, compromised values, and forgotten kids—the purported
objects of their passion.

Because superintendent turnover is so rampant and because
the stakes of turnover are so high, the most valuable asset a
superintendent candidate can offer is a transparent record of
success—a record verifiable through local sources, not spit-shined
on a platinum resume with letters of recommendation that recast
shortcomings as successes. Every school deserves a leader who
stakeholders know first-hand has a deep commitment to community. They need someone at the top who will stretch the buck
but not the truth, who won't be distracted by more lucrative
offers, who won't wither under stress, who knows how to
compromise and foster relationships, and whose foundation is set
with cast-iron integrity. Such a candidate will not gush about
passion, success, and commitment. These qualities will be etched
quietly in the dignity of the candidate's life, readable to all.

Cathy Harlow embodied these qualities. She did not absorb her
leadership capabilities through osmosis, even though she worked
closely with me in a mentorship relationship for many years. That
the Tyrone Area School District had achieved the holy grail of
educational return-on-investment—graduating seniors for two
consecutive years with the state's highest academic growth while
maintaining a tax burden within the state's lowest percentiles—is a
testament to an administrative team on which she played no small
part. As a vital member of that team, she had always had an innate
ability to balance competing financial and personnel interests. I
empowered her to make bold management decisions. When many
young Tyrone teachers fled to neighboring school districts to escape
non-competitive salaries during the last decade, she consulted with
the board to broker revolutionary salary and benefit proposals that
stopped the hemorrhaging—without raising taxes. Her manner with
staff was unswervingly courteous and respectful and her service to
the taxpayer and to the student was indisputable. Those wise
enough to confide in her discovered a human touch not common in
the world of cold financials.

If Cathy learned anything from her extended mentorship, it
might be this truth about longevity: that it is as valuable as it is
maligned. While longevity is scorned in the cut-and-run era of
CEO's, it is the guarantor of continuity in a successful school.
Wall Street-traded cyber corporations like K12 Schools aside,
schools are not businesses to be overhauled by hatchet-wielding
CEOs who slice their way to artificial markers of success through

swift cuts and trendy practices. Yet somehow as a member of the administrative team Cathy had overseen a faculty reduction of 13% during a two-year, statewide funding crises. As a result of surgical cuts initiated by capable building principals and the curriculum director in conjunction with Cathy, it was nothing short of genius that student growth during this period actually increased, as opposed to the state and national trends.

Cathy Harlow helped us to achieve this growth because she knew that productivity in a school started with knowing people well—their strengths, wants, weaknesses, and fears. This step alone takes years to accomplish (some never accomplish it with their own families). The short-lived superintendent rarely accomplishes it, nor do they see a need to. But the leader with a long-term commitment knows that this people knowledge—some call it emotional intelligence—is crucial in making people feel valued to carry out an enduring vision even in tough times. Such a leader will walk in her staff's shoes long enough to make sure her vision is legitimate and possible. Only then can a school leader achieve lasting excellence.

Though she approached the job from a non-traditional business background as a CPA, she walked more miles in the shoes of staff members than many were aware. She observed teachers in their classrooms for weeks at a time—longer than had some of the building principals responsible for teacher evaluations. What's more, her own volition Cathy had directed clubs and taught courses in our schools, experiencing the craft first-hand so that she could freshly understand both its challenges and triumphs. Because of these experiences, she had no misconceptions about educational theories—and she was less inclined to brook poor excuses for failure. How different she was from the pretentious ranks of research-steeped administrators. Cathy knew bogus educational theory when she saw it, understood the limitations of impractical, ivory-tower research that supported such theory, and recognized (as too few in educational leadership do) that all that glitters does not produce practical results. She valued instructional data—but only as far as it offered direction and explained results. She knew that learning was a gradual, recursive process. In an age of NCLB data-driven madness, she had the common sense to know that weighing the pig would not make it any fatter—only the quality of the feed (great instruction) could do that.

When board members consider a superintendent, they try to look into the soul of each candidate—a slippery, non-scientific proposition. In her soul, many on our board sensed humility, genuineness, integrity, wisdom, compassion, and selflessness. Such soul-readings are always sketchy with an outside candidate. But with Harlow we had a keen mind capable of grasping both the large and small of school operation. Through all of the political and educational crises detailed in this book, her first question was not "What's the cost?" but "How will this benefit students?"

The board searched for someone who might do better—some wanted a candidate that would not do "business as usual." But weighing the top-of-the-state return-on-investment that Harlow and our staff had helped to secure for both the taxpayers and the kids in this district, the board majority understood that our "business-as-usual" was far from the usual.

The politics of grooming Harlow and installing her as my successor were controversial from the get-go. I harbored no illusions about this whatsoever. Some especially questioned Harlow's qualifications because she approached superintendence through the business end. Despite the prevailing opinion that she could outshine most job candidates in every business and human relations respect, she had never completed the required three years of teaching stipulated in 24 P.A. Section 10-1003 and 22 P.A. Section 49.14 of the Pennsylvania School Code. In conjunction with the board, we pursued a path around this hurdle.

By 2008, the Broad Residency Program in Urban Education on the national level had opened alternative routes to the super-intendent position, placing 110 residents in executive positions in more than thirty-five districts and charter management organi-zations. We determined to meet with Secretary of Education Gerald Zahorchak to seek a waiver for the teaching requirement. Zahorchak wrote a letter to the Board on April 28, 2010 indicating the Department of Education approval:

> [PDE] has determined that the District has met the legal requirements of the Empowerment Act. Therefore, it is my pleasure to inform you that the Department has approved the District's [waiver] request . . . If appointed by the Board of Directors, Cathy Harlow will be issued a conditional letter of eligibility for the limited purpose of establishing her eligibility . . . as Chief Executive Officer for only the Tyrone Area School District and only in the Commonwealth of Pennsylvania.

Harlow's path would by no means be easy; she still had to enroll in a state approved Letter of Eligibility program in the spring of 2008 with a course-load of 18 annual credits while completing her district duties full-time. Additionally, she had to participate in PDE's Inspired Leadership Program and satisfy its core standards, spending up to 20% of her weekly activities during the school year engaged in learning and observing standards-based systems in action at the classroom and building levels. Her evaluation had to be submitted to PDE annually, and by March of 2010 she had logged hundreds of hours of classroom observation and 60 credits at Penn Educational Leadership—essentially a full-time student, an employee, and a mother no-less who managed a 3.9 GPA.

Others saw this tangled route as a plus. In her persistence, she proved her mettle. Cathy's desire to improve her mind was evident in a tireless regimen of continuing education classes leading to a Ph.D., and yet her coursework never interfered with her business administrator duties. On the contrary, it was recognized among staff that to get something done, you spoke to Harlow. Harlow had been in Tyrone to oversee every computer and book purchased and to see every program and brick in the district set. As part of a skilled team of professionals and community supporters, she guarded each dollar dedicated to each brick as if it were her own. She cared about the lives that depended on those dollars and those bricks and understood the gravity of the superintendent's responsibility.

But that did not allay the critics. In a January 8, 2008 *Altoona Mirror* article, at least one director sneered at the waiver process in the press:

> School board director Ray Detwiler said it looks more like Miller is trying to handpick his successor. "It's not fair to anyone," . . . Detwiler said the program is not a model, just a way to stack the deck and squeeze out other candidates.

In a way, Detwiler's charges were reminiscent of the old charges of a "Miller Dynasty" prevalent with the Tom boards of the 1990s. Even though my son Norman, who was then a possible candidate for the superintendent position in neighboring Altoona, had no interest at that time in succeeding me in Tyrone, there were whispers of my engineering and exerting some brand of monarchical domain over the district after my departure. There were widespread whispers of Norman's return to Tyrone to lead, but those were ill-informed rumors at best. I had no inkling of his wanting to work at Tyrone in any capacity; that aside, it was wise to segregate the Miller name from the school district. He eventually secured a position of command as Assistant Superintendent in Central Dauphin School District near Harrisburg. It was tough for some folks to acknowledge that Harlow was simply the best candidate suited for the job and that I recognized her superiority as much as anyone who had worked with her closely on the board. Despite the fact that I mentored Harlow as my father had mentored me, there was nothing dynastic about her ascent—no pseudo-bloodline perpetuation scheme, no blinders-on loyalties. She worked her tail off. She managed virtually all superintendent-related tasks with vigor and precision. She was simply the best—an opinion vetted by an extensive interview process and a panel of interviewers culled from a representative sampling of stakeholders that included the entire community, which was encouraged to complete an online survey detailing the characteristics that they most wanted to see in a successor. Harlow fit those characteristics superbly, as many of them emphasized people-skills and intangibles as well as business acumen. Though we did not perceive classroom knowledge as an Achilles heel, we had created a new curriculum director position after eliminating the assistant superintendent position to help bolster and direct the instructional plan of the district. A former Tyrone middle school teacher and Dean of Students, Leslie Estep was exceptional in this regard.

While I did not disguise my support of Harlow under the scrutiny of motives, I also knew that any attempt to squelch her detractors would only jeopardize her chances. It was a political balancing act, for sure. Many genuine and well-meaning folks suspected that Harlow's business background was superlative, but they felt a degree of angst over her lack of classroom experience. Former Altoona teacher Larry Meckes expressed this view in a letter to the editor of the Mirror on January 22, 2008:

> I don't doubt for a minute the qualifications of [Harlow] as the business manager . . . However, schools are, or should be, run by educators, not moneymakers . . . There are many, already qualified people to fill the vacancies in educational administration within the area without having to create a waiver for someone special.

Even Harrisburg seemed against the idea. You can imagine our devastation when on May 2, 2011, Ron Tomalis, newly appointed Republican Secretary of Education under the Corbett Administration, informed us that "Under the current law, I have no latitude to waive explicit requirements of statute and regulation such as the ones at issue here. Therefore, I am not at liberty to grant the Letter of Eligibility you have requested for Ms. Harlow." This was purely political in my mind—a knock at the authority of out-going Democratic Secretary Zahorchak. It was little consolation that Tomalis indicated that PDE would soon endorse legislation that would allow the type of "mandate relief" we were seeking—soon to be known as Act 24[12]. I traveled to Harrisburg to meet with Tomalis to determine what in his opinion Harlow should do in the interim. She exceeded his recommendations, proceeding with a self-initiated, hands-on regimen of advising high school clubs and teaching an accounting course at the school to better apprise herself of the classroom and to experience the daily struggles and joys of both students and school staff. Eventually, after another round of snares and detours, Act 24 allowed her application for certification to be approved.

As with so many of my struggles detailed in these pages, patience, persistence, and perseverance carried Harlow through. At the opening ceremonies for the 2013-2014 school year, she surreptitiously secured a pair of my black wing-tips to use as a visual aid before the entire staff, quipping that she had impossibly large shoes to fill. At this printing, she has already—within the first year of her tenure—settled a contentious year-long teacher's contract dispute, resolved numerous disciplinary hearings, recommended a school budget for 2014-2015 with no tax increase, transferred a million dollars from the general fund to the capital reserve fund for future district maintenance projects, and survived heated school board meetings about a certain high school coach from Altoona. There are no shoes large enough that Cathy Harlow cannot fill, as long as she remembers the simple lessons of this book.

Principles of Prevailing

✓ Decades of successful policies, practices, and results can vaporize under the heat of a new administration's ardor; attention must be paid to the politics of transition.

---

12 An alternative path to obtain a letter of eligibility for a superintendent's credential.

- ✓ Beware the résumé-building candidate eager to hop on to a more lucrative gig in suburbia—and the one attached to a long-suppressed ideological agenda or vendetta.
- ✓ The most valuable asset a superintendent candidate can offer is a transparent record of success—a record verifiable through local sources, not spit-shined on a platinum resume.
- ✓ Embrace alternative routes to the superintendent position.
- ✓ While you need not disguise your support for a successor, know that any attempt to squelch detractors will jeopardize your goal.
- ✓ Be a conscientious mentor to those who may replace you.

To Harlow and to all brave souls who answer the call, including my own son Norman Miller, I wish you Godspeed.

Bibliography

Andrekovich, Tim. (2011, April 5). A personal e-mail to Senator John Eichelberger.

AP News Service. (1999, August 25). "Former governor urges financial vigilance". *Reading Eagle.*

Artman, William Edgar. (1972, February 9). A letter to Governor Milton Shapp."

Asbury Park Press. (2009, December 12.) "PA public school salaries, 2007-08." *app.com.* Retrieved from http://php.app.com/PAteachers /search.php.

Bissinger, H.G. (2000). *Friday Night Lights.* Cambridge: Decapo Press.

Black, John A. and Fenwick W. English (1986). "The Lunatic Fringe: Prudes, Censors, Wackos, and Birchers". *What They Did Not Tell You In Schools of Education about School Administration.* Lancaster, Pennsylvania: Technomic Publishing, Co.

Bock, Greg. (1990, January 15). A letter to the editor. *The Tyrone Daily Herald.*

Bock, Greg. (1992, April 17). A letter to the editor. *The Tyrone Daily Herald.*

Bock, Greg. (2008, January 8). "Tyrone top job search mulled." *Altoona Mirror.*

Bolman, Lee G. and Terrence E. Deal. (2001). *Leading with Soul.* New York: John Wiley and Sons.

Brown, Faith. (1990, November 12. (A letter to the editor). *The Tyrone Daily Herald.*

Bucsko, Mike. (1997, November 16). "Residents attack school board over investments with Black." *The Pittsburgh Post-Gazette.*

Carolus, Rob. (2000, December 5). "Closure . . . vindication." *The Tyrone Daily Herald.*

Court of Common Pleas of Blair County, Pennsylvania. (1999, July 30) Docket No. 1999-03899. Class Action No. 98 GN 2603. Settlement Agreement Tyrone Area School District and Mid-State Bank & Trust Co, Keystone Financial, Inc.

Crosby, Shane F. (2013, September 9). A letter of complaint to William N. Miller from the Governor's Office of General Counsel.

Diane Ravitch and Rick Ayers in association comments on the *Saving Superman* film.

Education Commission of the States. (2001). "Transformational leadership: overcoming the constraints of the superintendency." *scrnexus.com.* Retrieved from http://www.srnexus. com/.

Education Writers Association. (2013, August 25). "Effective superintendents, effective boards." *ewa.org.* Retrieved from http:// www.ewa.org/docs/leadership.pdf.

Einstein, Albert. (1931). *qotd.org.* Retrieved from http://www.qotd.org/search/search.html?aid =143&page=12.

Families for Quality Education. (1993, May). Paid advertisements from Families for Quality Education. Altoona, Pennsylvania: WRTA radio station.

Faulkner, William. (1950, December 10). Nobel Prize acceptance speech delivered at the Nobel Banquet at the City Hall in Stockholm.

Fisher, Marc. (2013, April 1.) "The master." *New Yorker* Retrieved from http://www.newyorker.com/reporting/2013/04/01/130401fa_fact_fisher.

Franklin, Benjamin. (1730). "Apology for printers."

Franqui, Angel. (1992, May). "A letter to Reverend Donald Campbell."

Gandhi, Mahatma. (1925, October 22). *Collected Works of Mahatma Gandhi Vol. 33.* Publication Division, Ministry of Information & Broadcasting Gov. of India.

George., Camille. (1998, April 6). A letter to Superintendent William N. Miller.

Gerlach, Harry K. (1972, March 21). A letter to William Edgar Artman.

Gibbons, Mike. (2014, February 9). A letter to the editor. *Altoona Mirror.*

Hafer, Barbara. (1999, February 10). A letter to Dr. William N. Miller.

Heeter, Nate. (2013, June 24). "SAT scores by state 2012." *commonwealthfoundation.org.* Retrieved from http://www.commonwealth foundation.org/policyblog /detail/sat-scores-by-state-2012.

Herbert, Frank. (1990). *Dune.* New York: Ace Publishing.

Jackson, Barbara Loomis. (1995). *Balancing Act: The Political Role of the Urban School Superintendent.* University Press of America.

John's Blog. (2011, March 31 and October 13, 26). Retrieved from *senatoreichelberger.com.* http://senatoreichelberger.com/category/blog/.

Le Carre, John. (2013, September 5). "John Le Carre." *johnlecarre.com.* Retrieved from http://www. johnlecarre. com/.

Lewis, Kathryn. (1992, April 27). (A letter to the editor). *Altoona Mirror.*

Lord, Rich. (2013, September 1). "Donations from ex-cyber school raise concerns." *The Pittsburgh Post-Gazette.*

Lubienski, Christopher and Sarah TheuleLubienski (2006). "charter, private, public schools and academic achievement: new evidence from NAEP mathematics data." University of Illinois at Champaign-Urbana National Center for the Study of Privatization in Education.

Machiavelli, Niccolo. (1984). *The Prince.* New York: Bantam.

Madonna, Terry. (2011). Opinion Research Omnibus Poll.

Mains, Nathan. (2014, September 26). "Pennsylvania students outperform the nation on 2014 ACT." *The Tyrone Daily Herald.*

Meckes, Dan. (1992, April 28). "Clowns." *The Tyrone Daily Herald.*

Meckes, Larry. (2008, January 22). "School not in big business." (A letter to the editor.) *Altoona Mirror.*

Merryman, Richard. (2011, November). "New day to dawn for the TAHS career and technology and education." *TyNotes.* Tyrone, Pennsylvania: Tyrone Area School District.

Miller, William N. (1998, February 19). "Tyrone Area School District position paper on alleged Devon fraud case."

Morrow, Karen. (1992, April 15). A letter to the editor. *The Tyrone Daily Herald.*

Network of Concerned Citizens. (1992, May 30). An advertisement in *The Tyrone Daily Herald.*

(Redacted).(1981, April 10). A letter to the editor. *The Tyrone Daily Herald.*

(Redacted). (1988, May 5). "Tyrone's one man board." *Altoona Mirror.*

(Redacted).(1990, February 5). A letter to the Honorable Governor Robert Casey.

(Redacted).(1990, March 16). A letter to TASD Board President James P. Kimmel.

(Redacted). (1999, July 30). "Deposition summary of (redacted), former school director of the Tyrone Area School District." Prepared for Betts Law Offices by Jeffery E. McFadden, counsel for Mid-State Bank.

"Pennsylvania Act 195." *Ballotpedia.* 2015. Web. http://ballotpedia.org/ Pennsylvania_Act_195_(1970).

Pennsylvania Department of Education. (2013, January 2). "Data and statistics." *pde.org.* Retrieved from http://www.pde.state.pa.us /portal/server.pt/community/data_and_ statistics/7202.

Pennsylvania Football News. (2013, November 22). *pafootballnews.com.* Retrieved from http://www.pafootball news.com/.

Pennsylvania Value-Added Assessment System. (2012, November 20, 25). Retrieved from *PVAAS.org.* https://pvaas. sas.com/.

Pennsylvanians Opposed to Vouchers. (2011, February 5). "A news release from Pennsylvanians Opposed to Vouchers." Retrieved from *psba.org.* http://www.psba.org/issues-advocacy/issues-research.

People's Choice, The. (1993, October 30). "To the voters in the Tyrone School District." *The Tyrone Daily Herald.*

Pittsburgh Business Times. (2013, April 5). "Pennsylvania's top ranked school districts." Bizjournal.com. Retrieved from http://www.bizjournals.com/ pittsburgh/slideshow/2013/04/05/pennsylvanias-top-ranked-school.html?s=image_gallery&img_no=86.

Public School Code of 1949. (1949) "Manner of election or approval". Section 1073.

Reagan, Ronald. (1981, January 20). "First inaugural address: January 20th, 1981."

Reeves, Rick. (Station Manager).(1992, April 23-24). "Tyrone School Board." Altoona, Pennsylvania: WTAJ-TV Studio.

Rodkey, Randall. (1990, March 2) A letter to (Redacted).

Rotherham, Andy J. (1997, December.) "The test of sound public policy." *aasa.org.* Retrieved from http://www.aasa.org/SchoolAdministrator Article.aspx?id=15504.

Ruskin, John. (2013, November 12.) "John Ruskin and poems." Retrieved from *litera.co.uk.* http://www.litera.co.uk /john_ruskin_and_ poems/.

Russell, Stephen. (1997). A letter from Pennsylvania School Board Association's Chief Counsel.

Shakespeare, William. (2013). *2 Henry VI,* 4.2.59 in *The Complete Works of Shakespeare.* London: Longman.

Shakespeare, William. (2013). *The Merchant of Venice,* Act 2.7 in *The Complete Works of Shakespeare.* London: Longman.

Sites, Woodrow. (2011). A statement regarding proposed Senate Bill 1 presented on February 16, 2011 to The Pennsylvania Senate Education Committee.

Slekar, Timothy. (2011, November 22). A letter to the editor. *Altoona Mirror.*

Smith, Neil. (1991, May 3). A letter to the editor. *The Tyrone Daily Herald.*

Smith, Virginia. (2013, December 2). A telephone interview.

Smolin, Melanie. (2012, January 31). "Military gives 'F' to online education." *takepart.com.* Retrieved from http://www.takepart.com/article/2012/01/30/should-all-high-school-diplomas-be-treated-equally.

Sullivan, Ronald. (1966, April 20). "Foes of rising Birch Society organize in Jersey." *New York Times.*

Swift, Jonathan. (2013). *The Prose Works of Jonathan Swift, D. D., Volume IV. fullbooks.com.* Retrieved from http://www.fullbooks.com/The-Prose-Works-of-Jonathan-Swift-D-D-3.html.

Thatcher, Margaret. (2013, April 8). "Thatcher's quotes sting, startle and stick." *usatoday.com.* Retrieved from http://www.usatoday.com/story/news/world/2013 /04/08/thatcher- quotes/2062835/.

"The Horace Mann Sexual Abuse Scandal Is Even Worse Than We Thought." *Refinery29.com.* May 27, 2015. Web. http://www.refinery29.com/2015/05/88146/horace-mann-sexual-abuse-update.

Tomalis, Ronald J. (2011, May 18). A letter to Dr. William N. Miller.

Tutu, Desmond. (2000). *No Future Without Forgiveness.* Toronto: Random House.

Tyrone Area School District. (1991, April 2). "Report of the Tyrone Area School District Library Review Committee." Tyrone, Pennsylvania. William N. Miller.

Tyrone Area School District. (1992, January 17) Transcript of Rosalind Tate's Job Interview.

Tyrone Area School District. (2012, July 2). "Class of 2012 senior survey: a confidential report of unedited written comments as submitted by students compiled by Tyrone Area School District superintendent's office." Tyrone, Pennsylvania: William N. Miller.

Tyrone Daily Herald. (1992, May 18). "Bury the Hatchet." An unattributed political cartoon.

U.S. News and World Report. (2010, December 28) "U.S. News and World Report's America's best high schools" *usn.com.* Retrieved from http://www.usnews.com/education/best-high.,schools/pennsylvania /districts/tyrone-area-school-district/tyrone-area-high-school-17387.

Vergil. *Æneid,* (2001). translated by John Dryden. Vol. XIII. The Harvard Classics. New York: P.F. Collier & Son, 1909–14; *bartleby.com.* Retrieved from www.bartleby.com/13/.

Vonnegut, Kurt. (2013, January 5). "Vonnegut NEWS" *vonnegut.com* Retrieved from http://www.vonnegut.com/news.asp.

"Weingarten Rights Law and Legal Definition." *Uslegal.com.* 2015. Web. http://definitions.uslegal.com/w/weingarten-rights/.

Wells, Chiffon. (1992, May 17). "Tyrone area schools under 'moral' rule." *The Altoona Mirror.*

Werner, Virgie. (1990, April 10). "Book review committee, school board hears PSBA legal representatives." *The Tyrone Daily Herald.*

Werner, Virgie. (1993, May 21). "TASD Superintendent accused of violating district's political policy." *The Tyrone Daily Herald.*

Wunder, Bill. (1972, March 15-June 1). "Tyrone teachers talk." *The Tyrone Daily Herald.*

Yeager, Cynthia A. (2011, July 15). A letter to TASD Board President Lee Stover.

Zahorchak, Gerald L. (2010, April 28). A letter to TASD Board President Lee Stover.

Index

CPSIA information can be obtained at www.ICGtesting.com
Printed in the USA
BVOW11*0110121015

421061BV00003B/4/P

9 781620 066232